Follow the Path with Heart

By

Pamela Stowers Cunningham

For Bill, Michael, Logan Michelle and Eric

Table of Contents

Introduction... 5

Okies... 8

My Mother, Helen Corrine Elmore Stowers....... 13

Joanne "Frone" Ellison Pegler......................... 16

4:44 a.m.. 19

My Sister Patti.. 23

My Son Tommy... 30

Mike and Sauce Dunking............................... 35

I Was Thirteen.. 40

Me an Alcoholic? 47

1981... 53

Peter D. Stevens..57

Bryan Neubert..59

Margaret Ed.D.. 67

Louie.. 71

The Malibu.. 75

"Singing Seven Spanish Angels"..................... 78

Mice, Painters and Termites.......................... 81

Yard Sales... 83

Table of Contents, Continued

Bathrooms and Sunny D also Kleenex and Bras………………………….………………… 86

Bus Stops and Diamond Rings……………..…… 88

Coconut Crème Pie…………………………….... 91

God Minutes and "A" Types………………………96

Asphalt Meditation…………………………..…… 99

My Orange House……………………………..… 102

Ramblings of a Looney……………………..…… 103

The Titan II Missiles……………………………… 107

Roll Top Desk…………………………………….. 109

Toby………………………………………………… 110

Boulders………………………………………. 112

A Fib……………………………………………….115

Grief and Luggage………………………………118

Suicide…………………………………………...120

Crossroads………………………………………. 124

A Long Day……………………………………….. 128

Falling……………………………………………... 133

Jet Trails………………………………………….. 136

Table of Contents, Continued

Forgotten Grandmother...............................	138
Adventurous Girl...	141
Penn Park..	143
The Corn Festival..	145
Disneyland..	147
The Catalina Island Folding Comb.................	152
The Pacific..	157
El Pescador, Rosarito Beach, Baja, Mex...........	161
Ripley, Oklahoma.......................................	169
Albert Einstein..	175
Ceramics Can Cause Divorce......................	179
Achievements...	183
Hearthstone Park..	188
Valley National Bank..................................	192
Gifts by Nancy..	195
Windsurfing..	199
Barrio Hollywood.......................................	202
If you ride it, it will come.............................	208
The Ride for My Life..................................	213
Apache...	215

Table of Contents, Continued

The Desert Speaks…………………………	218
Sign……………………………………….	222
The Granny Trail………………………..	227
Follow the Path with Heart……………………	230

Introduction

It's June 5, 2016. Here I am at 4 o'clock in the afternoon pecking away at the keys. My friends think I should write. I call it the ramblings of a looney, but then that's a different story. I'm 72 years old searching for a way to express myself asking the same questions most seventy year olds ask. I'm looking at where I have been and asking where am I headed? I'll tell you where we're all headed; the grave. My skin knows this, it's sagging, skin hanging from breasts, stomach, arms and face. My breasts are hanging so low I may need a larger belt. Can't stand underwire bras anymore, they're too uncomfortable so I bought these little stretchy spandex ones that make my breasts almost look like they did back in the 70's when we all went braless and our sisters stood up straight.

I love wedge sandals with my skirts and pants. Slowly my style is changing from fashion to comfort. I swore I would never dress like "those old ladies." Yet, in the winter I wear Sperry Topsiders (I have three pair); in the summer I wear flip flops, wedges and Clark sandals. I bought my first Muumuu I swore I'd never buy.

Arriving home from my trip to town to our rural neighborhood in Vail in my semi-fashionable outfit, the transformation begins. The first thing I do is to take off the bra, the wedge sandals, and my jewelry and put on the Muumuu I now love. I feel like a rural, aging stripper, but a comfortable one.

I'm sure my life isn't any more interesting than the next person; it's just different. Let's face it, we've reached the summit and we're moving downhill and picking up speed. Ever notice how the week flies by from Monday to Friday? One of the benefits of being seventy-two and having grey hair is that you can say and do anything you feel like doing and don't give a damn if anyone likes it. Young men open doors for you and offer to carry your groceries. I say, "Your mother would be proud of you. Thank you." Back in the days of the Women's Movement I would have called them a male chauvinist pig. I've mellowed with age like cheese mine is no longer extra-sharp. It just doesn't matter anymore. I just want to have fun. I'm not worried about dying. The fact is none of us are getting out of here alive. We might as well have one hell of a time!

There are and have been remarkable people in history, literature and the arts. Yet, not one of them has lived the life of Pamela Stowers Cunningham; only I have. Like everyone else, my journey has been an interesting adventure; fraught with hilarious events, sadness, fear, loss and joy. I know where I have come from but I don't know where I'm headed. I'm writing my book of memoires because after all, I'm not getting any younger. I want to remember my life, my adventures, my accomplishments and the people who significantly affected my life and the world I live in. Writing about it must be the solution!

Okies

Tornado alley best describes my personality. Stillwater Oklahoma, part of tornado alley, was my birthplace as it was for most of my family. Mother, Dad and three grandparents were born in Oklahoma. That qualifies us as Okies. Much like a tornado I have a volatile temperament which is easily provoked by not getting my own way. On the other hand I am bright, funny, adventuresome, kind and tenacious. These traits led me to people along the way who inspired me in ways that changed my life. A friend described me once I get hold of something, "I was like a freight train traveling in a downhill tunnel picking up speed." My stubborn nature resembles someone trying to push a 1,000 pound bolder uphill. When it finally mows me down I'm flattened but get back up again. Hopefully not leaving any destruction on my way.

Although it wasn't always that way. But for many of my adult years from age twenty-five on, I led a reckless double life. Certainly I don't blame this on my family. Sure there were problems in my family, but there were also secrets.

For instance, we all knew Grandpa Stowers hid whiskey bottles all over the place. Under his car seat, in his toolbox and next to his night stand to name a few. Sometimes he was very antisocial, at other times he would be vain. He and grandma didn't have much money yet Grandpa had to have the best Florsheim shoes, Pendleton shirts and a pigeon blood ruby ring. Grandma on the other hand lived a little more within their means; she had to.

My father was a heavy drinker but he crossed the line somewhere into alcoholism after my brother died. I remember seeing his car crashed into a chicken coup in South Tucson on the front page of the *Arizona Daily Star*, our local newspaper. We all thought it funny at the time. Later I didn't think so.

My double life started somewhere in the late 60's and early 70's. I was a middleclass housewife, two children, nice house, my own car, checking account, yet I was restless and had a nervous disposition. I suffered from bouts of depression and anxiety. What seemed to give me a sense of ease was alcohol. Imagine pouring alcohol, a depressant, on top of depression.

I suffered from loneliness far from my home in Arizona. There were only eight or nine house on our little street in this small country town of Rock Tavern New York. The only business in Rock Tavern was a "Rock Tavern." The countryside was like looking at a Norman Rockwell painting. Rolling hills scattered with working farms appeared around every turn in the road. As beautiful as it was, it didn't fill that empty void of loneliness. Then one day something wonderful happened. A woman and her family moved in next door. I noticed right away her British accent. She was born and educated in England and married to an author. She and I hit it off right away. She liked coffee, not tea. We spent many hours in her kitchen drinking coffee and talking about the loneliness we both felt married to husbands who were career driven, yet absent much of the time. Career widows we called ourselves.

She and her husband loved to entertain some of their friends from New York City who would drive up and stay for the weekend. They usually included us. Fondue parties were the rage then. The table would be covered with fondue pots of melted cheese and wine, Tempura for shrimp and vegetables and bottles and bottles of wine usually chosen by the host. He was a connoisseur of sorts. At least he fancied himself that way.

By ten o'clock we, as the British called it, were thoroughly pissed. We would either play endless charades or attempt to put together 1,000 piece jigsaw puzzles. We thought it was fun but there was only one problem; I was pouring alcohol into a little alcoholic in the making.

It wasn't long before my friend and I were picking dandelions in the yard for whipping up batches of dandelion wine. Only a few miles away the Brotherhood Winery, one of the earliest in New York, held its Saturday wine tastings. They would give you a tiny complimentary wine tasting glass to sample the variety of wines. My friend and I kept moving to the end of the line to start all over again. When you finished the wine tasting you entered a room where bottles could be purchased. At the end of the table stood a large coffee urn where you would fill your tiny complimentary wine glass with coffee. I guess the winery thought that would sober you up. Looking back I find this idea totally ridiculous but it made sense at the time.

When we returned to Arizona my drinking escalated and so did my harmful behavior. I needed a way out of the insanity. I am so grateful I was lead to a program of recovery for alcoholics and that I have a disease called alcoholism that is treatable as long as I don't pick up a drink. I soon discovered I was not a bad person trying to get good, I was a sick person trying to get well. Today I am 30 years sober and I have found a life better than I have ever imagined. But this is only a small part of my story. There is so much more. If I knew then what I know now I would be amazed how even the worst events of my earlier life would contribute to the interesting person I have become. But, I have heard it said, "Life is to be lived forward and understood backward."

My Mother, Helen Corrine Elmore Stowers

Like me, my mother had a nervous disposition. She was a real go getter. I learned from the best. Friends called her "Hurry Helen" because she never walked anywhere, she scurried. When we walked together she always walked faster than I. I didn't know if I was slow or she was just trying to get away from me.

That woman was talented in so many ways. Growing up on a farm in Ripley Oklahoma she learned to work the fields with her father Orville Renig Elmore. His friends called him Renig. I discovered many men in Oklahoma go by their middle names, a tradition very confusing to me except I married a man from Northern California who was known in his childhood as Douglas yet his first name was William. Years later he called himself Bill. By the way, many Oklahomans migrated to California during the Dust Bowl Days. Maybe the name thing was a trend imported from the Okies.

My family's work ethic was engrained in me. Great Grandpa Elmore, my mother's grandfather, was in the Oklahoma Land Rush and homesteaded a quarter section for the farm. Her dad worked the farm until he retired. Mother was right alongside him. They also survived the Dust Bowl Days. Grandma once told me she had to sweep the dirt out of the house several times a day because dust was everywhere and you couldn't see the blue sky.

My mother was a fine seamstress, a gardener with a green thumb, (Oklahoma farm roots), piano player, and the best pie maker ever. I look back and see that I acquired the same interests except I don't play the piano or have her green thumb. I kill a lot of plants.

She was tall, brunette hair and brown eyes but her most distinguished feature was her posture and long legs. After high school she went to Oklahoma City to Business College and modeled clothing in order to earn some money. Models learn to walk with a book on their heads. This became a curse for me as I grew up because she was always reminding to sit or stand up straight without the benefit of book.

What I remember most was her attire for gardening. It was the 50's in Southern California where we migrated from Oklahoma. On hot summer days she wore white cuffed short shorts, a halter top, two inch white wedge sandals with ankle straps and a chignon in her hair. Add a pair of sunglasses and she could have doubled as Ava Gardner.

My mother described me as an overly sensitive child who was prone to upset stomachs and crying. Still am. She called me the "Pepto Bismo" kid. She never told me when we were going somewhere because I would get an upset stomach. I took most things personally therefore my feelings were hurt easily. I was about to meet someone who would change my way of looking at life. Joanne "Frone" Ellison.

Joanne "Frone" Ellison Pegler

I first met Joanne when we moved to Whittier California in 1952, I was eight and she was ten. She came to my yard to meet the new girl on the block as the movers where unloading the van. She wore a floral printed cotton dress. She had probably worn the dress for a long time because it was too small and too short. Her hair had been recently permed and resembled a Brillo pad, and she wore maroon bedroom slippers. But the most distinguishing sight was the cast on her arm. I had never seen a cast before. Later I was asked to autograph it.

Joanne was the funniest person I had ever known. She could have been a stand-up comic. But her real gift was the garage talent shows she produced. For the mere cost of a penny you could see the two of us act out movies, pretending to strum an old guitar as we lip synced songs to 45 rpm records. We, of course, provided the little kids with popcorn.

We made up names for ourselves. Frone was a name I made up for her. Mine was Pamshna. These names made absolutely no sense at all. We did everything together: sang "Moonlight Bay" as we took turns washing dishes, in harmony of course. Sometimes on our walks to school we spent our milk money on Danny's glazed donuts. You could watch the baker fry the glazed donuts in front of a large plate glass window. Biting into a hot glazed donut was an experience to remember.

We always made our costumes for Halloween. But there was a Halloween that turned out to be the one from hell; one we created for ourselves. One year we made Rockette costumes with black sparkly top hats and canes. We also carried a can for donations to the <u>March of Dimes Telethon</u>, a fairly common practice in our neighborhood. On the way home that night we had a bright idea to go to the soda fountain and eat hamburgers, French fries, drink cherry cokes and play the jukebox with the money we had collected. Problem was a friend of ours saw what we had done and told our parents. Of course we had to pay it back. We must have babysat for six months. That is not the only time we got in trouble.

One summer at Huntington Beach Joanne and I rented some rubber rafts and paddled out quite far to catch the waves in. The tide changed and an undertow developed dragging us toward the barnacle clad pier. The barnacles would have torn us to shreds but fortunately a lifeguard swam out to save us. This is an experience I'll never forget.

Joanne and I have remained friends since 1952. We have moved to different parts of the country, I moved to Tucson and she moved to Hot Springs Village, Arkansas. For a long time we saw each other every year or so. Our children are grown and scattered to the winds. But she is still the funniest person I know and I am grateful to call her my friend.

4:44 a.m.

Military men bring home many of their daily routines even after the war is over. My dad was no exception. He taught my sister Patti and I how to flip a quarter on a tightly made bed, nurses corners, straight sides, collar at the top. On school mornings the wood floor would creak from the weight of him as he stepped into the bedroom. We would be awakened to the finest whistle of Reveille I have ever heard. Next, he would shout, "Its 4:44, time to hit the boards. Rise and shine!"

Dad could whistle anything, Big Band, Jazz and Classical. As he came in the front door after a day's work, he had a special whistle to let Mom know he was home. When playtime on the street at night was over he had a whistle for that. He never shouted our names. His whistle could be discerned from all the other parents'. How I miss that whistle. How I miss my dad.

Dad was a 1st Lieutenant Navigator on a B-24 Liberator bomber the crew named "Calamity Jane." His squadron was assigned to the North African Theater. The Navigator's table sat in the nose of the plane with his back to the two nose gunners. In one of the battles

Dad was hit with a piece of shrapnel that would have hit his heart except for the brass New Testament bible in his left pocket his sister Dorothy had given him before he shipped out. For this injury he received the Purple Heart.

When Dad was discharged from the service, the Army Air Corp they called it, he had experienced what all soldiers experience; fatigue and memories. Mom didn't want to talk about the war anymore but Dad did. He wanted to relive the times by going to endless war movies. I would go with dad as long as I was supplied with a cache of candy which, of course, I shared with him. When I look back now as an adult, I find it shocking that a parent would take a child to a graphic war movie. I never suffered the effects of those movies; I was just happy to be with my dad.

The opportunity and great thrill for Dad was in 1971 when he and mom flew to New York where I lived with my family. Next door was my best friend Jo and her author husband Keith. Keith's passion was World War II history. He and some of his friends played war games. One evening after dinner with my parents and neighbor friends, Keith asked my dad if he would be willing to tell him some of his stories. Like little children around a campfire, we all sat on the floor surrounding Dad in his chair listening for hours to the retelling of his war stories. He was in hog heaven! None of us realized how therapeutic this was for him. Mom, on the other hand, sat on the other end of the living room remembering the agony and fear she experienced back home wondering if she would ever see him again.

After the war Dad moved us around looking for work. We went from Stillwater Oklahoma, Galveston Texas, Whittier California and eventually Tucson Arizona. Dad was an accountant, a very good one. His reputation preceded him. Most of his clients were small business people who admired him for his humor, kindness and excellent service. Word spread in many of the minority communities. His Mexican and Chinese American businesses grew by word of mouth. I didn't realize until recently after reading some of the letters dad had written during the war that he studied physics, calculus and mapping. Only a seasoned accountant would prepare his profit and loss statements in fountain pen.

My dad's Army photograph hangs in the hall, his purple heart in my cedar chest, and his letters to my mother in perfect cursive penmanship in a box in my office. It's been many years since the war. What I remember most about my dad was his sense of humor, his whistle and the love he had for my mother.

My Sister Patti

My sister Patti has always spelled her name with an "I". She was rebellious from the start. She is almost three years younger than I so we had different interest and friends. We didn't do much together unless it was with the whole family.

It wasn't always that way. As small children we played together all the time with our dolls, on swings in the backyard and dressed up in Grandma's clothes, but Patti always had a doll in her arm. Mother usually dressed us alike until grade school. She taught me to match my skirt, blouse and sweater. I would look all put together, Patti on the other hand had her own style ideas. One morning Mother was having a terrible time getting her to change what she wore. Along with a floral summer blouse she wore a plaid wool winter skirt; she dressed the way she wanted mismatched and all. Mother decided to let Patti's hair grow long so she could make braids tied with plaid taffeta bows and full set of bangs which nearly touched her eyebrows.

Patti hated shoes. She wanted to go barefoot all the time. Teachers from her elementary school would call Mother to tell her that one more time they couldn't find her shoes. It was hopeless. She was a strong minded tomboy through and through.

Patti made many friends easily. I on the other hand had one best friend, Joanne Ellison. One of Patti's favorite things to do was play at Georgia Cranston's house. Georgia's mother was an uptight interior designer living in a modest little subdivision house. She didn't want them playing inside unless they sat and played dolls or read books. Backyards and barefoot won out!

When we were very young we had large Mama Dolls with wooden arms, legs and head, and little squeak boxes inside that when tipped over would say, "Mama." One day our dolls were sitting on little Mexican chairs under our bedroom window when the rain got them wet and ruined Patti's doll. I'm sure she played with dolls after that but she would rather have run around barefoot and play outside. Grandma used to call her a little rascal after the Our Gang kids on television.

One Easter, Mother decided to give us perms. We looked like little dolls in polka dot pinafore dresses with Brillo pads on our heads. How embarrassing! While at Huntington Beach that summer we contracted lice. Imagine having small metal combs pulled through permed hair? It was excruciating!

Patti and our little brother Mike were close. I was older and doing my own thing. One of my favorite pictures of her is posed with Mike on his new bike.

In 1958 when I was 14, we moved from Whittier to Tucson Arizona, Patti was 11 and Mike was 6. Patti made friends easily. Mother said she attracted every underfed, neglected kid in the neighborhood. She would often drag some poor kid home for dinner. I can remember her saying to Mother, "Please mom, can she stay for dinner, she hasn't had anything to eat today." Mother would always give in because she too was a compassionate person. After our brother Mike died, our family sort of scattered to the winds. Patti drifted to all her friends for support and understanding. All those friends were there to support her. I became the parent.

Sibling feuds were no different than any other family. We argued over who was to wash dishes, whose turn it was to set the table, make the beds, use the phone, ad infinitum. I remember the night we got into a physical fight tearing buttons off each other's' pajamas while screaming and wrestling on the floor. Mom came bounding into the bedroom, "That's it!" she said as she left the room. "I have had it with both of you. I don't care what you do to each other!" I don't remember us having a fight after that.

We both were sent to Catholic high school after Mike died. While in high school Patti got pregnant and was sent to a home for pregnant girls who would give birth and put their babies up for adoption.

I was working at Motorola Semiconductor in Tempe at the time and was able to pick her up on Sundays to go to the movies. When time to give birth grew near, she and I created a signal when she was going to the hospital. When I got my signal call from her I went to the hospital after work to find her crying in her bed. "They never let me see my baby and I don't even know what sex it is," she said. She was devastated. It was painful to see her so sad. I snuck a wheelchair into her room and waited until the nurses left the area, rolled her to the nursery window and looked in.

There wrapped in a pink blanket was the only baby without a name. On the bassinet a little sign read, "Baby Girl." Poor Patti my heart broke for her. At only seventeen years old she had gone through what many grown women experience. I rolled her to a phone booth so she could call our parents. It wasn't long before the nurse found us. What could she have done that would have been worse than what Patti already felt. All she wanted was for her big sister to be there with her.

After graduation she was pregnant again. She headed to Northern California to stay with our Aunt Dorothy and Uncle Burt until her baby was born. She made a decision to give him up for adoption too.

Patti eventually returned to Tucson but not before she married a violent man who beat her even when she was pregnant. One day I remember helping her run away from him. There were many more life threatening events before she finally divorced him.

After her son Tim was born they headed to the Southern California. One weekend she and friends traveled to Rosarito Beach in the Baja where she met her husband Lynn. South Laguna and Capistrano became their home for many years. Their successful rug cleaning business continued on in Rosarito Beach where they retired.

In 1999 our mother was diagnosed with Alzheimer's disease. Patti and I had been estranged for almost eight years when I got the call from her telling me mom had fallen and broken her hip. I remember sitting in my car outside the hospital crying for an hour knowing she would never go home again. I lived so far away it was a blessing to have my sister manage Mother's care. She died in Rosarito Baja Mexico on March 29, 2004.

I watched my sister go through many health challenges including removal of a cancerous kidney, recovery from Hepatitis C, and the death of Lynn. After his death and the recession her business income suffered. In her faith and support she gets from her fellow church members, neighbors, friends, trusted employee and family she is able to succeed.

In 2015 I asked my sister to come for a visit to our home. Patti had not been to Tucson since 1988 and had not seen her nephew Mike. It was so heartwarming to see my little sis and my son Mike eating and laughing together. I fed her favorite green corn tamales for breakfast, lunch and dinner from Lerua's Mexican Restaurant.

By the way the daughter who helped pay for her trip back to Arizona was the little "Baby Girl" she had given up for adoption. Christine located Patti several years ago through the search for her birth mother. They were reunited and now Christine and her husband Mike bought a house in Patti's neighborhood. Oh, and the other baby she gave up for adoption was found by Christine. Patti and her son Brian were reunited a few years ago. I have a beautiful picture of Patti and her three children. Her babies came back to her at last.

My sister and I have not always been real close. Patti has overcome loss, serious health, and income issues but she is not just a survivor; she is a bright light in the lives of many people because of her generosity and friendship. We have sometimes long periods of estrangement, but through God and our combined faiths we are able to communicate in a way we never did before. Life is picking up speed the older we grow and I would like to spend as much time with my sister as possible before one of us goes, which inevitably we will. She is the only person left on this earth who shares our common memories. I love her very much. There's no need in asking why so late in life? "Better late than never".

My Son Tommy

In the spring of 2014, April 5th to be exact, my eldest son Tommy was on business in Africa as he often was. He was CEO of a private aviation company. He traveled the world, but on this occasion he was in Malabo, Equatorial Guinea. The hotel manager where he dined said Tommy had arrived early that evening for dinner with friends. He took Tommy on a tour of his hotel then had drinks with him in the lounge. Throughout the evening there was talking and laughter when suddenly one of the men came running up because "Someone had collapsed." It was Tommy.

On April 5th in Malabo, Tommy died of sudden cardiac arrest. They tried CPR for over a half hour before the ambulance arrived but he was already gone.

Tommy died doing what he loved to do. His passion for aviation and his integrity in the business developed success. He was funny, bright and compassionate. He made many friends in the aviation industry. He was married to his wife for almost 12 years. Their anniversary would have been a month later. Her birthday was two weeks after he died. Death has no compassion.

What makes this story remarkable is that Tommy and I had been estranged for seventeen years. In July of 2012 we reconciled and talked quite often for the next eighteen months. On Friday, May 10, 2013 we met for lunch at one of his favorite restaurants called Mama Louisa's. He learned to love Italian food at home when he grew up. (His other favorite Tucson restaurant was Lucky Wishbone Chicken). He shared his "Joe's Pasta Special" with three cheeses and spicy sauce. He ordered a Dr. Pepper; my favorite. I'm sure my gray hair was a shock to him as his loss of hair was to me. He was a middle aged man and I was a grey haired advanced middle aged mother. We knew each other and yet we didn't.

We talked about this and that but I noticed he had tears in his eyes. I knew if I touched him he would burst out crying. He was a lot like his mom in that respect. So, we looked at pictures of his dogs, edgeless pool and others. I noticed he had on a navy blue polo shirt with his company logo on the sleeve; a picture of a jet pointed toward the sky with double parentheses on both sides. He formed the company in 1998 at Scottsdale Airport in Scottsdale Arizona. He specialized in the sale and charter of executive jets. Over the years he had the privilege of providing charter service to Executives, celebrities, Heads of State, and dignitaries.

We talked about his start of an Organ Recovery Team. Organ recovery teams transport by jet the organs harvested from a dying patient. The team then transports the organ to the recipient. He had held a conference with first responders who had committed to the team. They included doctors, nurses, firemen, and EMT's. He had come to Tucson for the purpose of organizing the team. After his death I was able to see his beautiful emergency ambulance with the company logo on the side along with the words, "Organ Recovery Team." The tragic coincidence occurred to me recently that when he died in Africa he was unable to donate his organs to save someone else. The Organ Recovery Team will continue in his honor.

The last time we spoke he was returning to Malabo via Paris. Once he emailed me a picture of himself standing with the lighted Eiffel Tower behind him. I cherish that picture. It was taken on Valentine's Day, two months before he died. Our last phone call was on March 27th on his way to Malabo. It would be his final trip. May 10th was the only time I saw him.

After I left the restaurant that day, I had to pull off the road because I was in a state of shock. It seemed almost surreal. To this day, I can see him walking away from me at the restaurant headed for the cashier. I remember everything he had on but I cannot remember the details of his face. I have pictures of him throughout his life including one the Malabo business hotel sent me of his last Christmas standing in front of the tree in his navy blue business suit and tie looking like the picture of health. I have had to quit asking why this happened but how do I live with purpose for the rest of my life despite the loss. A close friend said, "Honor his life by celebrating yours. God isn't through with you yet!"

There were a number of condolence cards I received but one in particular came from a young man who heard my story. He wrote inside a card with a black and white profile of the Buddha on the front. It read, "May the memories of your son Tommy illumine your path wherever you go." I have passed this quote on to others who have lost love ones. Talking about him with people is what I want to do more than anything but people don't know what to say. I learned two important things to say: "What was your loved one's name; and, tell me what you remember most about them." I have seen grown men break down and cry when I ask those questions because that's what they most want to talk about. It really works!

Since Tommy died I have been searching for something that would fill the void left by his death. Some of my friends suggested I write.

A friend of mine gave me a framed cross stitch which read, "Who I am is God's gift to me. Who I become is my gift to God." I always liked that. I hope he isn't disappointed. I would like to believe I haven't totally screwed it up. Certainly the birth of my two sons was the highlight of my life. I have been married three times, the first to my sons' father, the second a younger man, and my current husband Bill is a man I didn't pick. God did. I believe Tommy would have liked Bill. I didn't mention that Bill is six foot three, but Tommy was six foot five.

Mike and Sauce Dunking

My son Michael John was born October 22, 1966, a year after his brother. Following a toddler and carrying a baby is exhausting work. As Mike became a toddler himself it was something only a parent of two boys a year apart can know. Needless to say it was a real challenge for me. Oh how I loved being a mom. The endless diapers, potty training, vomit, split lips, endless clothes shopping, picking up toys, and cleaning green beans and squash all over me, the floor and the table.

Trips to the grocery store were fun. I would put Mike in the baby seat and Tommy in the basket. By the time we finished shopping Mike had the store's complimentary cookie crumbs all over his face and Tommy had opened his dad's package of salami.

In New York winters the parking lots are covered with frozen ice and pot holes. Unlike Arizona where they offer to help you to your car, New Yorkers ignore you. Now comes the nightmare. Trying to navigate the cart full of groceries and kids across the frozen parking lot was like dodging land mines. It's a miracle we ever made it home in one piece.

Tommy and Mike were best friends. As Mike puts it, "Tommy was my first friend." Like any second child, I rarely had time to follow him around taking volumes of pictures as I did for my first child. Parents take thousands of pictures of their first child but if the next one is a year later, you are so tired from chasing them around all day photography is the last thing on your mind. You are lucky if you have one hundred pictures by the time they reach high school. Most of the pictures before that are of the two of them. Poor Mike, there are rarely any photos of him alone. I suppose I could crop some old photographs so they could be only of him.

Mike was a sweet child, beautiful smile and a love for his big brother. He learned most of his early behaviors by observation. He also inherited all of his brother's hand me down clothes. But, somewhere along the line his true personality came out. Researchers say that second children are the social ones. I believe in his case this was true. He made friends easily whereas Tommy was content by himself. Tommy was a leader in a group, Mike a follower. Sometimes this lead him to some troubled companions. Despite the divorce and summer school, Mike graduated from high school.

After high school, Mike moved out of the house and took odd jobs until he landed a job as a framer for a home builder. He was good at his job. One of the many things I can say about Mike, he is a hard worker. Mike was in and out of my life for many years. I never knew where he was or when he might reappear. My fear was that he had died. Every once in a while he would call or show up somewhere. But, most of all he was a vagabond trying to find his way.

In 2001 Mike finally called me. His girlfriend's mother had died. Before she died she told Mike, "You go see your mom before she is gone." He called me the next day. Shortly thereafter he and his wife Echo were married and became a part of our lives. A few years after they were married they decided to have a baby. Logan Michelle was born September 10, 2005; son Eric born December 7, 1989 is an Army Green Beret. Becoming a grandparent was Mike's finest gift to us.

Visits once a month on Sundays meant Italian sauce, meatballs and Italian sausage; Mike's favorite. I received the recipe from the mother of a high school friend whose mother learned to make the sauce in her Italian in-law's New Jersey restaurant. My recipe is on a little tomato stained 3 x 5 index card dictated to me in her mother's kitchen. When I make spaghetti and meatballs and sausage the family gets to dunk a chunk of French bread into the sauce; it's a family tradition. Anyone who comes to the house on spaghetti night gets to dunk the bread.

Mike has become a devoted husband and father. He not only helped Echo raise her two daughters Lacey and Jessica, he is involved with Logan's school, sports and church. He volunteers wherever he can to help others. It isn't unusual to find one of his hand built creations in someone's yard. He built a wall in our patio for Bill's workroom and tools. When Logan and her older sisters were raising pigs for 4H, he built a pig trailer for the group. I can't even start to list all the pieces of Mike's construction that are scattered around town. He is a fine carpenter. I'm so proud of Mike and his commitment to his family.

The loss of his brother hit him hard. He wouldn't talk about it much. But one day visiting his house he gave me some pictures he thought I would like of Tommy. This was his way of saying, "Mom,

I lost Tommy too but I'm still here and I want you to be happy." I'm so grateful Mike is in my life again. Any time he wants spaghetti and meatballs I have it covered. I also make Mike's favorite coconut crème pie from the recipe my mom gave me.

I Was Thirteen

When I was thirteen I was thin, cute and wore a pony tail. Like most of the girls my age, pony tails and Mamie Eisenhower bangs were the style. Circle skirts with poodles (why poodles?) on them and Alice Lon crinolines (very full petty coats made of yards and yards of net). Crinolines were worn under full skirts to make them stand out. We wore silk neck scarves, sweaters worn backwards and buttoned up the back and saddle oxfords with Bobbie socks. We, in my opinion were adorable. Alice Lon, by the way, was a woman Lawrence Welk danced with on his show. When she was twirled, you could see her different colored crinolines.

Shirley B, a girlfriend who lived next door, had crinolines of every color she wanted. Her mother Flora made them on a treadle non-electric sewing machine. Shirley was spoiled rotten and always wanted her way but she always acted well when she got it. When she didn't, she was a brat. We all tried to look like Shirley including myself. She was three years older than I, Joanne was two and I was a thirteen year old freshman the year my Grandfather Stowers molested me.

My best friend Joanne would occasionally spend the night at my Grandma and Grandpa's house. They had a little apartment behind the garage; two bedrooms, a laundry room and a bathroom. We slept in one room and Grandpa in the other. We believed what we were always told that he slept out there because he snored too loud. I'm sure there were other reasons but we were kids and wouldn't understand.

Grandpa was an alcoholic. He drank Old Grandad whiskey. He hid his bottles everywhere. Under the seat of his car, in his tool box and next to his bed. Joanne's dad did the same thing. When we first met, Joanne was living down at the corner of the block in an old house built in the 30's with a basement. It was her grandma's house. One day, we went on a hunt for the bottles. She showed me so many places. One behind the stove in the kitchen, one in the laundry closet, one under the mattress and one in a drawer. We thought it was funny. We don't any more.

I loved to go to my grandparents' house. Grandma made our favorite food and made sure we ate my favorite silver dollar pancakes served with real butter and maple syrup in a little tin log cabin when tipped poured syrup out the chimney. Placed at the end of her stove we ate our pancakes at a little dropped leaf chrome, yellow top table with two chairs. My pancakes had to be golden, not too brown. I can see her standing at the kitchen sink beating the hell out of the batter. One time I asked her if I could do it, but she said, "Pammie, you go get the step stool so you can watch Grandma do it." She measured the flour and cornmeal by her hands, a pinch of salt, a couple of spoonful of bacon fat, and a pinch of baking powder. Hands and fingers were her measuring cups and spoons. The pancakes were always the same. Perfect! If I had a dollar for every silver dollar sized pancake I ate, I would have enough today to buy a little table and chairs; they wouldn't look like hers.

It was shortly after 8th grade graduation one summer when Joanne and I went to Grandma and Grandpa's house to spend the weekend. For graduation I had received some luggage, a turquoise G.E. transistor radio the size of a large cell phone and some hot pink baby doll pajamas. Portable radios had just come out of production and were the latest thing. I packed my new pajamas in my new little overnight bag along with my transistor radio.

Joanne and I would lay in the old brass bed, next to a mirrored vanity. Large white roses covered the walls in paper my grandmother had hung. Next to the bed was a large screened window that faced the alley way. Grandma had planted a honeysuckle vine next to the window and on warm summer nights you could smell the blossoms. I loved that room. The mattress was soft and the pillows were feather. Hopes and dreams were planned in that room.

The alley was one of my favorite haunts as a young girl. There were adventures at every house on either side of the alley. Mrs. Wilson had chickens and the lady next door had boysenberry vines that grew along her fence on the alley side. I would try to quietly sneak by, grab some berries undetected and run. Apparently her kitchen window faced the alley. I swore she must have lived in that kitchen because most of the times she would catch me. Across the alley was a family with a bunch of wild ruffian kids. They used profanity and at the time I didn't know what profanity was. That's where I learned to say the word shit. I was probably six years old. Later that day I got home and couldn't wait to share the new word I learned; it was not met with the reaction I hoped for. As the Ivory soap scraped across my teeth, my mother's angry voice said, "Don't you ever use that bad word again, and don't talk to those kids!" Lesson learned at least for a very long time.

At the end of the alley was the magical avocado tree when climbed to the top there appeared a little bent chair shaped branch where the queen sat and reigned over all and a salt shaker was a necessary piece of equipment used to sprinkle on the avocados. I can see to this day every place on that alley. Even when I got much older, Joanne and I would walk down the alley and repeat the same adventure I took as a younger child. We would make up wonderful stories about the alley. It was a safe wonderland where we could get away from the world of adults. When I look back now, it has a deeper meaning.

That summer night after graduation Joanne and I were getting ready for bed. I put on my new hot pink baby doll pajamas I was so proud of. Joanne and I went next door to grandpa's room to say goodnight. Joanne said goodnight and returned to our room. Grandpa took hold of my arm and asked me to stay a minute. I could smell the whiskey on his breath. He didn't have on his glasses so he looked different. He scared me. He didn't let go. Instead he reached up with his other hand and fondled my right breast and said something to me I don't remember. I left the room confused, shocked not knowing what to think. When I told Joanne about it she said, "Oh, my dad does that to me all the time." We both laughed but deep inside our young teenage minds something felt all upside down and uncomfortable. It wasn't until I got much older and went to therapy I was able to retrace my life and see how molestation by someone I trusted affected my life for a very long time.

I didn't know that girls who are molested by family members develop low self-esteem. They often become promiscuous and look for love and approval from men. Many turn to alcohol or drugs to try to numb the memories. The problem is when you sober up or end the affair with the man you think understands, the memories, pain and shame are still there. The empty hole inside you is eroded deeper and deeper. It is only through recovery the hole is filled with something greater than shame, low self-esteem and self-contempt. For me it was a Higher Power and the program of recovery.

Through the certain steps I learned to forgive Grandpa if I wanted to be happy and serene inside. I learned to forgive myself for all the things I did as a result of my molestation. Today, I love my life and wouldn't want to change anything. It is because my past allows me to reach other broken women who want to let go of the one hundred pound baggage off their backs in order to be free.

Me an Alcoholic?

My life and my circumstances are wonderful today. I have a terrific husband, a nice home and the respect of friends and family. But it wasn't always that way.

I grew up with loving parents, a home and all my needs taken care of. Life was good and I was pretty happy despite the death of my brother Michael when I was fifteen. I went to a college prep high school, Salpointe Catholic High School, graduated in 1961 with a "B" average and met some nice friends. I dated several boys in school, but met a young man four years older that I at a CYO (Catholic Youth Organization) dance at St. Joseph's Church. He was from Kansas and graduated from a military academy. He was a good boy but he couldn't dance worth a damn. After all, dancing was a huge part of my social life. School dances after the game were part of high school in the late fifties and early sixties.

I dated Roy through some of my junior year off and on because I wanted to date other boys in my school. The same thing continued in my senior year but after graduation we became more serious. He told me he wanted to marry me so like any good Catholic couple we attended pre-canna courses for engaged couples to prepare them for marriage. The only kind of birth control the church allowed; the rhythm method. The rhythm method requires you chart your period each month, add days after you stop to determine when you ovulate and can get pregnant. During that time you have to abstain from sex. No condoms or birth control pills were allowed.

After graduation I got a job working in my dad's accounting office and Roy joined the Navy because his job prospects in Tucson were slim in the excavation business. Off he went to basic training and I worked and went out with my girlfriends. Roy was a nice guy but he was missing something. When he came home in June on leave from basic training we took a drive out in the desert and had sex. I was a virgin. I was seventeen years old. We must have been in the safe period because I didn't get pregnant, thank God! After that we decided we would abstain until marriage.

He returned to active duty and I continued my job and having fun with friends and one of his sisters. The Air Force base hosted Friday night dances for the airman with an open invitation to young women in Tucson. This was when you could drive on to the base without any problem. So off Nancy and I went to just dance.

After the dance started, Nancy and I left for the Ladies Room. On our way back from the dance we were walking by the airmen's T.V. area when a good looking man with dark brown hair smiled at me. Our eyes met and we held it for a second or two but in that amount of time something happened that I had not experienced before; electric attraction. I remember everything, I wore a pale blue velveteen dress and black suede shoes. He wore a dark green sweater over an oxford cloth shirt topped with a trench coat. I could hear the music off in the distance. It seemed like time slowed down as if I was walking in slow motion.

Returning to the dance, I saw him again. This time he was in a suit and tie, the dress code for dances. I turned away and asked Nancy, "Is the boy in the suit and dark hair coming our way?" She said "Yes, and he is headed for you." I felt a soft tap on my shoulder, turned around and there he stood smiling with a twinkle in his eyes that I had never seen before in any boy. He introduced himself, "I'm Ed would you like to dance?" " The way he held me, the way he danced was very East Coast. I found out he was from New York. We danced the rest of the night away.

He asked me for my phone number and if it was alright to call me because he wanted to see me again. Because it was December and the holidays he left for Phoenix to see his mother and little brother. Before he left he gave me a beautiful Christmas card I still have in my cedar chest. I am a hopeless romantic despite the divorce. We danced in my parents living room to Elvis Presley's "It will be a Blue Christmas without You." We dated from then on. In July of 1962 he proposed to me. On December 29th, 1962 we married.

One August day we were invited to a wedding for one of his buddies. After the wedding we all gathered at the home of the bride. The small adobe house had no air conditioning other than a swamp cooler. Monsoon season in August is hot and humid often hitting one hundred degrees or higher. We were all hot and thirsty so the host was serving us little pitchers, not glasses, of beer.

Between the Mexican food and the beer, I got drunk. I was wearing a pink linen dress with shoes to match with salsa and beer down the front of the dress. Needless to say, Ed had to take me home like that but not before one of his buddies gave me a habanero chile to sober me up. One bite and my mouth was on fire, in fact I couldn't catch my breath. My first drink was my first drunk.

This was to continue for many years. I did not know then what I know now, that when you pour alcohol into an alcoholic it triggers the disease and they are off and running until it takes about everything in your life.

I lost a marriage to that guy I met at the Air Force Base after nineteen years of marriage and two sons. I wreaked havoc in his life and lives of our sons. I also lost my self-respect, dignity and grace as a woman. My alcoholism had progressed to the point of no return. I was beyond human aid. I felt like I wanted to die because the emotional pain and hopelessness were so bad.

In 1984 a family member was being treated for drug addiction and the treatment center suggested family members go to recovery programs that would help us too. Little did I know my life was about to do a one hundred eighty degree turn. I sat in meetings with other people like me and learned about alcoholism and a solution that worked for them to not drink one day at a time. They demonstrated through their own experience the steps I could take to not only stay sober but be happy and useful to others.

    My family and I have been closer than ever. I stayed sober through the death of my mother and of my son Tommy, and that in itself is a miracle. I earned a college education, retired from my career at the University and met my husband Bill. Through sobriety my dignity, grace and worth as a woman have been restored. Today I feel like I can be helpful to others who don't want to drink anymore. I look back over my drinking history and see how far down the scale I went before I got desperate enough to want to change. I have been sober now thirty years and have found a life so much better than I could have ever dreamed. So, yes, I am grateful to be an alcoholic in recovery because my dark past can be my greatest gift if it can help someone see a way out of the madness of alcohol. I found a way out because someone reached out to me and showed me the way.

1981

The spring of 1981, talk about a tornado! Ed had left me for someone else and I was left with two sad, angry abandoned teenage sons. God how I hated what they had to go through. Life with Ed had become unbearable. I didn't leave him for another man but I had become an angry, depressed, unhappy woman. We were no longer best friends. We had become combatants in a world that appeared normal from the outside but was a war behind closed doors.

There were loud fights in the yard at night and shouting matches in the house in front of our sons. There were "right fights" where nobody wins, infidelities, name calling and putting each other down in front of our sons. Both of us had turned outside our marriage to the person we thought understood. In most cases all they wanted was sex. All I wanted was love.

I had been seeing a Vietnam vet at our racquetball club before Ed left. Ed had already met his wife to be. The vet, whose name I have long forgotten, lived with his brother who was a drug dealer. I was meeting at his house for sex and pot. At home I felt unloved, unwanted and alone. I can't believe how selfish and self-absorbed I was. My poor sons had an absent dad and a mom who was not there for them. I was in the thralls of ensuing divorce after Ed left and this guy was trying to be there for me. In looking back, he was only interested in a roll in the hay.

In June I was notified of my high school twenty year reunion. I took the vet as my guest on Friday night, but on Saturday I went alone. I met with my three best friends who I hadn't seen for quite some time. We were having the best time drinking and dancing. I, of course, was drinking them under the table. I was also dancing with a man I had known back in high school whose family was quite notable in Tucson. He asked for my phone number and told me he would call me.

The reunion ended late but in my inebriated state I decided to stop by my vet boy friend's house. We were having drinks in the kitchen when his brother came in with a couple of joints. He handed me one and I took a hit. I don't remember much after that except I was in and out of a black out. I was blacked out just enough to see the brothers rape me. I know today the joint must have been laced with a knockout drug. Years later when I got sober I learned I would never have been there if I had not been drinking. Drinking had taken me to the lowest place in my life.

By July Ed asked for a divorce. Anyone who goes through a difficult trial divorce knows what hell is. But, I got through it and the boys continued in school and spent time with their friends at the racquetball club. What they didn't know about that night from hell was their dad was sitting in the carport when I got home at 2:00 a.m. He was parked facing out. When I got out of my car, he grabbed me and drug me into the house. I don't remember what he said but he threatened to beat me unless I had sex with him. So I did. I didn't know until years later that that was rape too. That's why I call it the night from hell. I never want to forget where alcohol took me. I lost everything that night; my dignity, grace and worth as a woman and I gave it away.

Today after thirty years of sobriety and working a program my dignity, grace and worth as a woman has been restored. My life has been turned around by the loving grace of God. We have a saying, "No matter how far down the scale we have gone we see how our experience can benefit others." This has been true when working with alcoholic women who have gone through hell themselves. To see a woman grow and be restored into the woman God wants her to be is a joy I would not want to miss.

Peter D. Stevens, Cowboy

One cold morning in Sheridan Wyoming, a seven year old boy named Pete while rummaging through the garbage was discovered by a Cheyenne man and his sons on horseback. Pete had run away from an abusive home so the "Old Man" put Pete on the back of his horse and took him home. The Old Man adopted Pete into his family and treated him like another son.

Over the years Pete became a cowboy but was sidelined by a broken foot. The doctor on hand never set it right so Pete had a stiff foot and never walked normally again. This didn't stop him from pursuing an interesting life of adventure. After his foot healed, he traveled the rails for years working odd jobs here and there. The people he met were "Bo's" on their way somewhere.

After he had settled in Northern New Mexico he picked up carving little wood "Santos", little saints standing in chapel boxes. He would bury them in the ground to give them the look of antiquities. We met years later after he moved to Tucson. He had become a master carpenter and only sold his furniture pieces to a well-known Gallery. When he knew he was dying he called me one day and asked me if I liked the seven drawer high boy he had made? I told him I had always wanted a high boy. He said, "I'll sell it to you." I said, "I can't afford one of your pieces." He asked what I was willing to pay so I told him exactly what I had in my savings account. He said, "It's yours." I still have that little hand carved high boy chest of drawers with his name carved in the back.

Pete changed the way I looked at myself and the world around me. He died in January 1995 of lung cancer. I used to tell him that he made a difference in my life and he would just laugh. After his friends found out he was dying the single thing they told him was that he had made a difference in their lives. I got to say, "I told you so!"

Pete had many quotes. Two of my favorites are "Whether a man says he can or he can't, either way he's right" by Henry Ford. "A warrior takes action despite shaky knees." Author unknown.

Bryan Neubert

"Excuse me, my luggage didn't show up on the carousel," I said to the America West Airline representative. "May I see your ticket please," she said. "Ma'am your ticket is for Southwest Airlines, this is America West Airlines. Check their carousel." The Reno Nevada Airport was relatively small with only a half dozen carousels but there across the luggage area on the last carousel was my brown Samsonite suitcase and my maroon saddle bag.

Bryan Neubert's summer horse camp would be starting tomorrow morning early and with no clothes, saddle or bridle, I would have had to observe and not participate. As it turns out I was looking in the wrong place. What a relief. I picked up my rental car and with my saddle, luggage and sense of relief I headed for the parking garage.

Alturas California is in the upper north east corner of California close to the Oregon border. From Reno it is close to a three hour drive. I couldn't wait to get to Bryan's horse ranch for the chance of a lifetime for someone like me who at fifty came to the horse world totally inexperienced. Bryan is one of the premiere trainers of natural horsemanship. Over the years I had attended his clinics at the J6 Equestrian Ranch in Benson Arizona. He was famous in several countries for his gentle, effective method of developing trust with the horse. He could start a colt in less than an hour.

As I drove into Alturas I was surprised to see a very small town with one main street and an intersecting street adjacent to the railroad tracks. The main street has several stores, restaurants, gas stations and convenience marts. Prior to the trip I had looked on the Internet at the Alturas Hotel photos so I recognized it immediately. It was a quaint white two story hotel with red trim. On the second level there was a large veranda where you could sit and enjoy the activity below on the street. Inside it had deep red carpet and a polished mahogany registration desk.

The desk clerk said the elevator didn't work so I would have to carry my luggage up without the assistance of a bellboy. It was time to cowgirl up and drag my saddle and suitcase up the stairs. Customers had the choice of a room with bath or a dorm room with a women's community bath. The bath had several private shower and toilet stalls and a long mirrored vanity. It wasn't fancy but then I was going to a horse camp not a prom. You can't expect the Hilton for the reasonable price I paid for five nights.

Sparsely decorated would be an understatement for my room. It had a small bed, a small dresser, one small chair and nightstand and the smallest closet I had ever seen. The room must have been designed for a child not an adult. Oh well, who cares! I was about to experience a chance of a lifetime to attend Bryan Neubert's Horse Camp.

After getting myself unpacked and settled, I had time to take a drive out to the ranch just to familiarize myself with the area. I had entered rural America. Ranches and farms framed the winding road like a Currier and Ives painting. I came to a fork in the road and wasn't real sure of which way to turn. I noticed a family in their driveway so I drove up to the edge of the yard and asked how I could get to the address I was seeking. A friendly man said, "Oh, you're here for Bryan's Horse Camp." How did he know? I found out later at the hotel Bryan was the most famous man in town. He was also one of the nicest people you could meet.

A dirt road off the main road led me to the gate of the ranch. The overhead sign read: "The Neubert Family." Greeting me at the gate were two or three mares and a curious young colt. It wasn't until the next day at the start of the camp that I finally saw the number of horses on the ranch. I returned to town, ate some dinner and turned in early for the big day.

Monday morning after breakfast I returned to the hotel to load my saddle and tack for a trip to the ranch. The agenda for the day was colt starting. Most of the colts had not been ridden before. I was assigned a young gunmetal quarter horse gelding I named "Gunny". That wasn't his real name, just the one I gave him.

In the morning a couple of young friends and Luke, Bryan's son, drove the herd into a large circular enclosure with troughs. The horses had plenty of grass to graze on but this was a time for grain and supplements. Horses love grain, especially oats.

The Neubert's had three children who all worked the ranch and rode like the wind. His wife Patty was a gracious hostess and seasoned horsewoman. Their home was a true ranch home, country kitchen, fireplace and large kitchen table. Like most ranchers, during harvest or fouling season, most of the teenage friends of the family are enlisted to help with the fouling and chores. Bryan stands a beautiful red roan stud who has fathered most of horses on the ranch.

The morning arrived for our first class. Each student had a colt to start. Most of the participants brought their own horses. Bryan provided me with a colt that had been ridden a little but was still green.

The next day we taught the horse to back up from the ground. I would gently shift the halter back and forth across his nose and at the same time putting backward pressure on him for him to back up. I watched his eyes and ears waiting for the slightest backward shift of his weight releasing the pressure on the halter. I worked for quite some time but by the time class was over he was backing up with very little pressure.

Day three. As I haltered Gunny, I picked up the rope rein under his chin, he immediately backed up. I rubbed all over him and praised him for remembering. Next, the flag. The nylon flag is attached to a riding crop and is used to flag the horse to move. The more you expose the horse to moving the flag the more he learns to stay calm even through outside distractions that would normally spook him. You learn to get him to stand still even though you are running the flag over his entire body. It works, it really does. Next, I put a blanket, saddle and snaffle bit on the horse and prepared to ride him.

Now for round pen work. The round pen is a large circular paneled area ranging from fifty to one hundred feet in circumference. I applied the same technique used on the ground but this time in the saddle. It sounds funny but the horse doesn't know they can move with a rider on their back. The horse learned to follow my lead. I had to bump him several times with my feet. As soon as his weight shifted I released pressure from the halter. Little by little he was walking around the round pen. I got him to turn left and right easily with the traffic of all the other riders in the pen as well.

The next day we took the young colts out for a short ride on the ranch. What a thrill. In the afternoon I was given a big sorrel quarter horse for class. The group was led all over the ranch. We practiced walking over water, backing up a small hills and trotting with the group. While Bryan was instructing something I had already accomplished, I started riding down the hill. I didn't realize how far I had ridden until I turned around and saw the group at the top hill. Then it happened. I asked the horse to canter up the hill. It was my first time cantering and he performed like the pro he was. As I reached the top with the class watching me I yelled "Yahoo!" as my hat flew off. Everyone applauded and laughed as a real cowgirl was born. A young cowboy retrieved my hat. It was a great day!

Every day Bryan's wife Patti would provide us with a complete hot lunch. We were all real hungry because we had worked hard all morning. The comradery around the table was alive with people talking about what they were learning. I was the most inexperienced rider so it was all new to me and I loved every moment of it. Our last day we worked more on colt trotting and separating from the herd. Horses can get real attached to a buddy horse and want to be with him all the time. The horse is trained to rely more on its rider and less on his buddy.

That evening was our farewell dinner. As we sat around listening to Bryan talk about what we learned and recite cowboy poetry we had a short prayer service. I was filled with gratitude for what I learned at camp. As I took in the gorgeous sunset there were three deer who had come up to the pasture fence. It was if they came to listen to Bryan tell his stories. The day came to a happy farewell to all the students and one of the best trainers in the country.

When I returned home my horse thought he had a new rider because I brought all the experience and memories with me all tucked in the suitcase and saddle bag I remembered to pick up from the luggage carousel at the airport.

Margaret Ed.D.

Over the past almost thirty years of continuous sobriety I came to understand the meaning of the sayings, "The road gets narrower the longer we are sober"; and, "more will be revealed."

Let me say that I am not one who has drifted away from my recovery. I attend several meetings a week and work with other recovering women. That is why at nineteen years, I became baffled and leveled by depression.

I experienced bouts of it since I was a young woman, but marriage, a family and active drinking took the edge off for a while until I got sober. Then from March 2003 to March 2004 my mother died, my two twelve year old dogs died, I had an accident with my horse, and had some heart problems. By October I had hit a dark bottom and was starting to give up because it seemed so hopeless. I had all the symptoms of depression: fatigue, anger, acute sadness, and sleep problems. Everything had become an effort and I was losing interest in the things I loved doing.

I kept thinking if I talk about it in meetings, pray more, exercise more, eat right…on and on ad infinitum, I will be okay. Unfortunately, this was not the case.

I heard in meetings, "In our desperation is God's opportunity." Finally, one morning I got on my knees and surrendered to God simply saying, "God, I am powerless over this illness, please send help." The next day I got an e-mail "out of the blue" from my longtime friend who had moved out of state.

Now I had not intended to resume our relationship but I knew that she knew me better than anyone else, so I wrote telling her I was having a very difficult time. As usual, she asked me to write about it then e-mail to her. The depression was apparently jumping off the page because she called me at 3:00 a.m. to see if I was okay. She then did what a trusted friend does. She gave me some very strong suggestions to contact a doctor who I knew in the program who in turn directed me to another doctor in the program who was familiar with depression. Within 48 hours I was sitting in her office pouring out my story.

Today, I ask God "What do you want me to learn from the depression?" More will be revealed because I know from my journey in sobriety that God always takes what I perceive as a problem and brings some gift of good out of it, especially if it will help another suffering alcoholic. I know that more will be revealed, but I have to trust that it will be on God's timetable, not mine.

Not long after my friend called I contacted a doctor who referred me to Margaret, Ed. D. who became my therapist. She and I met for about eight years. Before she would work with me I had to see a Psychiatrist who could diagnose me. My diagnosis was Bi-polar II. After taking my prescribed medication it was if the blinders were taken away from my eyes and the world took on more meaning. My clarity returned and coupled with my sobriety, therapy and medication my life is almost normal. Margaret Ed.D was the psychologist recommended by my doctor.

What I liked most about Margaret E.D. was the way in which she would read to me her summary of our last meeting outlining where I was, what I talked about, the enthusiasm for my recovery and my progress. No one has ever applied their therapy in this manner.

Since Margaret retired, I am looking for someone who has similar therapy but I may not find someone like her because she was one of a kind. I never know who will appear on my journey. `Funny how life is to be lived forward, and understood backward.

Louie

I took two semesters of photography at Pima Community College taught by the late Louis Carlos Bernal. He had received a National Endowment of the Arts grant to complete a series on a* perspective of Old Barrios in Tucson. He was able to earn the trust and respect of the residents in their homes. His photographs were a stunning portrayal of their traditions and faith. The striking contrast of black and white echoed in their faces the life they had lived.

"Louie", we called him, was an excellent instructor of photography. He had a good sense of humor and took his art very seriously. We photographed in black and white because he believed it more clearly revealed the depth and shades that gave more life to the subject. We used traditional film cameras, loaded the camera in a dark room, developed, matted and framed our photographs. We began with photographing old wood branches or animal bones found in the desert, pictures of nature and a self-portrait. The self-portrait was not like the cell phone "selfies" today that everyone is obsessed with. Nor was it a picture someone else took of you. The self-portrait he wanted was a photograph that best reflected who we were at that point in our lives. At the time I was taking fine art classes: ceramics on the wheel, drawing, printmaking photography and basic design some of which were displayed in my photograph.

The subjects of my photograph were an easel on which a drawing stood, a photograph of my husband and sons (my husband had an Afro hair style and the boys were dressed in polyester), a camera, and a popular 70's bent chrome chair. A piece of my pottery sat on the floor along with some well-known self-help books: *I'm Okay, You're Okay, Open Marriage, Our Body Ourselves* and *Illusions* to name a few. On the chair was a favorite potted plant and a copy of *Better Homes and Gardens Cookbook.* All of these were an important part of my life at the time. Louie gave me an "A" on my self-portrait.

Digital cameras today do almost anything for you that were previously performed by hand. But it was the hands on film camera that required more tactile interaction with your work. It was challenging work but worth the outcome.

I love the unintentional surprises that sneak into the photographs. At my granddaughter's birthday she asked me to take a group picture of all her friends. Later, when I examined the photo I saw my son back in the kitchen carving a ham. My 10 year old granddaughter Logan is a real comic. Like many children her age they like to play the clown. Many of my pictures of her from age 8-10 show her making all kinds of funny faces when we are trying to take a nice family photo. No matter how hard we tried to get her to smile pretty, she continued the comic and sometimes distorted faces. Someday when she is a teenager and dating I will haul out the old photo album for her date to see. Grandmas can be comedians too.

Today is June 17, 2016. I'm drawing a blank today. Probably because I'm in physical pain. Every time I walk my mile I end up the next day with pain in my glutes and down my right thigh. My physical therapist gave me some exercises to strengthen my core. Is that like the middle of an apple? He told me I have to do these for the rest of my life. The exercises were designed to relieve my hip and glute pain created by my long drive to town. Now if I can only remember to do them. I like the quote, "Of all the things I lost in life, I miss my mind the most."

Sitting too long is the enemy of the elderly. If seventy is the new sixty why doesn't my body feel like that? In the morning I tell myself, "Jump up", but my body says, "No way." "Use it or lose it we say!" A close friend of mine told me I should look at the things that are still working, not the ones that aren't. I'm pretty lucky that I have good health in general but my friend doesn't. I feel guilty complaining to her because she suffers so much. I hate complaining when I have it so good. Then there is Louie. He's dead and I'm still here so what the hell am I complaining about?

The Malibu

Two years ago my husband bought me a 2014 Chevy Malibu. I love this car, it's white, sporty, fully loaded, and the wheels are pretty. The ambient lighting after dark is blue and turns the inside of the car into a romantic night spot. All I need is a disco ball. The stereo system is great, the backup video, OnStar and Sirius Radio are wonderful too. But the acceleration from zero to 60 is more than impressive; not that I am drag racing or anything, I just want to know that when I punch it I can get out of Dodge fast. Just because I'm seventy-two doesn't mean I can't appreciate a car with speed. I grew up around cars and boyfriends with cars and drag races, street races, pin stripping, metal flake paint jobs and souped up engines and learned to appreciate a fine piece of machinery.

For my husband it was the most expensive car he ever bought. One would think a Corvette or a Porsche would be considered an expensive car but not mine. You see last year we had a hail storm with hail the size of large walnuts that pummeled my new Malibu with the velocity you would expect from a shotgun. It was pitted all over the top of the roof, south side of the car and hood. We didn't have a carport or garage to protect it so I stood at my kitchen window crying as I watched my new car destroyed by the desert monsoon.

After the deductible was paid for the body repair we still had to lay out quite a bit of money. After 17 years of "thinking about it", which is what all engineers do before they make a decision, he decided to have a garage built. I don't think I mentioned the $1,200.00 in pack rat damage we laid out for leaving the vehicles out at night. With the cost of the Malibu and the garage combined, he bought the most expensive car he had ever purchased in his life. I'm not complaining, my sweet Malibu and Bill's truck now have a home.

We took an oath to never turn the garage into a storage shed like most of the neighbors have. Their garages are loaded with God only knows what and their cars sit in the driveway baking in the Arizona sun. Go figure. The only things in our garage besides the vehicles are the air compressor for the tires and a small handheld car vacuum for the interior, Bill's roping dummy and reata. Oh, and left over lumber from the construction of the garage. Now all we have to do is decide what we would like to build with the lumber. I'd like a picnic table and benches. I think we'll wait until the summer monsoon season passes. One thing is for sure. When I pull in the gate to our property, I hit the remote door opener to our beautiful garage where my sporty Malibu resides.

"Singing Seven Spanish Angels"

I remember the first time I walked into the living room of Bill's house shortly after we met. Everything was beige or brown. The curtains, the rug, and his recliner were brown with the exception of his off-white sofa and loveseat. What I noticed next was a signed print of a Jim Cox painting by the name of "Singing Seven Spanish Angels." It hung crooked in a thin snap on clear plastic frame with no matting or glass. It was a really nice print of a dozen or more well-known celebrity cowboys standing and some sitting around a campfire where a large cast iron caldron and a large coffee pot sat among the coals. One man had a guitar and the rest are singing. In the background is the "cookie" and his pantry wagon, behind him the Rincon Mountains.

The year after Bill and I got married I planned a surprise birthday party along with the newly framed and matted print. He hung it over the mantel and it is there to this day. That evening, one by one a friend would pop in unannounced, then another and another. It took three people arriving for Bill to figure out something was up.

We celebrated with cake and sang happy birthday. I recited the following poem I wrote for his special day:

Names

I met a man named Cunningham

He stands about six foot three.

I met him at a horse clinic eatin'

a sandwich under a tree.

Now names are often fittin'

they suite a man real well.

But this one takes the cake cause

it sure fills the *Bill.*

He stole my chair, he stole my

heart, in December he stole my name.

If that's not a *Cunning* plan by

A *ham* named Bill my mind is goin' lame.

I waited a few years before I imposed my decorating ideas on our house, but slowly one piece at a time I added a chair here and a lamp there, some new window coverings and some of my own furniture. Plants were added and some colorful art. One day Bill made the following comment: "This was just a house, but you made it a home." His remark meant a lot to me.

As the years passed we did some painting and redecorating. A few years ago I bought a Carol Griggs print called "Daughters of the Earth" of two Native American sisters on horseback. I took the print in to Lazy Boy Furniture and said, "I want to buy some furniture that tie into this piece of art." Before you know it I had a sofa, two chairs, a glass top coffee table and end table and an area rug that pulled it all together. It looks darn good if I say so myself. All that old brown and beige furniture has found a new home at the Goodwill.

As I look around the room I see that every single piece of Bill's furniture, drapes and carpet have been replaced with new things. The room is outlined in beautiful family pictures, art prints and my floral photography. Along with the artwork is a cat named Layla who has taken up permanent residence on the sofa, sort of a cat pillow. The one thing that still remains is the framed, matted print of "Singing Seven Spanish Angels" hanging over the mantel.

Mice, Painters and Termites

Did you know that mice like to dance at night? Well they do. I know because I was awakened one night by the sound of mice scurrying back and forth in the attic above my bed. They could have at least been considerate enough to find a dance hall at the other end of the house. "Critter Control" was called to come inspect our house. We had found a hole in the patio where there was an entrance to the attic. Did I mention that there was a two inch opening between the studs in the attic where mice would fall to their deaths? Once they fell down the wall they couldn't get back up. The smell of decomposition certainly wasn't Chanel No5. It takes about a week to ten days for the smell to go away. I think we ran out of at least one can of room spray, maybe two. Traps were set in the ceiling and all the entrances closed off. Four mice have already met their "Waterloo". The charge: $1,040.00. Now the termites.

A contractor was hired to paint the outside of the house for $1,700.00. In the course of painting the frames around the windows his brush punched through the frame and out came hundreds of termites. We called the exterminator to inspect our house and, of course, because of the age of our house we were convinced to have a major treatment. This meant that we had to move all the furniture to the middle of the rooms so that they could treat all the outside walls.

Now for people in their 70's this is not an easy job. Bill can't kneel on his arthritic knees and I can't do a lot of bending and lifting because of my bad back (an old horse injury). When we were finished we stood in the hallway crippled from the task and congratulated ourselves for not trying to strangle each other. I said to Bill, "Do you know what the hardest thing is about this?" He said, "My knees hurt?" No. "My arthritic hands hurt?" No. "Well then what, I give?" I said, "We have to move everything back." Needless to say I won't be cooking tonight. Just think, for all our labor we get to pay them a mere $900.00.

For all the jobs the grand total for the painting, mice and termites was $3,640.00. We could have taken a month long Alaskan cruise for that. The problem is we may have come home to a houseless cement pad. The horse would have been happy because he would had the full acre to himself and we would be sleeping in the horse trailer.

Yard Sales

I wish I could remember everything I'd ever sold in a yard sale. Certainly, I have been a customer at many, but I'm thinking more about the yard sales I have held over my life.

I don't remember having one until the mid-eighties. Vacation money had been stolen out of my home with no extra put aside for a long awaited trip. My second husband and I decided to hold a yard sale at his mother's house. She claimed it was more centrally located. I remember selling a bike I liked, an electric typewriter on which I wouldn't be writing this book, dishes, books, and other miscellaneous items. By some miracle we sold enough to take our vacation.

The next yard sale I remember was at the end of the second marriage. We needed to sell items too large to move into either my small two bedroom house or his not yet to be acquired apartment. Our entertainment center was very large as were our sofa, club chair and ottoman, dining room set, and king size bed. I'm sure there were many other items, I just don't remember their significance now. With the proceeds of that sale we repaired the air conditioner and roof for the new owners. We were on the verge of broke because my husband had been hiding some of his income and savings. It is water under the bridge now, but back then it seemed so important.

The final yard sale (I'm glad they didn't call it a garage sale because I didn't have one yet) was in the Barrio Hollywood when I had sold my house and was moving to Vail to marry Bill. Most of what I sold were duplicates. I sold an old T.V., a lawn mower I wouldn't need on desert horse property, some more dishes and pans, and God knows what else. There wasn't too much because the previous yard sale had weaned out the bulk.

The day after the yard sale Bill and three of his horse buddies drove their trucks and horse trailers to the barrio to load my belongings and transport them to Vail and to my new home. The trailers were packed full and ready to depart when I did one last walk through. There on my front porch was my beautiful euphorbia succulent next to the white clay greeter goose. I asked Bill's friend Joe if we had any room left? As he opened the door to Bill's trailer, there was a space just big enough for the plant. I left the greeter goose on the porch for the new owner.

Since I have lived in Vail we haven't had to have a yard sale yet. I've shopped many yard sales but don't look forward to the one we would hold here. It would mean either one of us died; or, we will both be moving because the property is too much to handle any more. One way or another we will have a yard sale, probably a big one. I don't think very much about it because either way it is a task too momentous to contemplate. Even though we have tried to simplify our lives, just thinking about Bill's workbench and tool room is too much. Thankfully he will have to take what he wants and sell the rest.

I don't have to worry at least for today about having a yard sale. The necessity will arrive soon enough. Until then we'll keep eliminating excess through donation to the Goodwill where our contributions will get a new life some of which may end up in someone else's yard sale. The reincarnation of stuff.

Bathrooms and Sunny D.

Ever notice as you get older, much older, your frequency of visits to the porcelain bowl increases little by little. When you are older and married, like college roommates' menstrual cycles, your bladders start to synchronize. My husband and I are no exception. We are fortunate to have two bathrooms because if we didn't he would have to keep an empty Sunny Delight bottle next to his bed like he did when we went camping.

Kleenex and bras ....

I have a habit of taking my bra off at night when I'm watching t.v. and tucking it along the side of the sofa cushion. I also do this with Kleenex. I like to write in a favorite chair but sometimes I'm on a roll and don't want to get up to get more Kleenex but I often find a used one tucked into the side of my chair cushion. You can usually tell where I have been by the trail of tissues I leave around the house. What is it about runny noses and getting older? The parts of the body you want to be wet are dry and the parts that you want to be dry are wet. I would just as soon not have to start wearing panty liners for an occasional leak when I sneeze. But my nose? Honestly I have gone through so much Kleenex I should take out stock in the company.

Back to the bras. I have several bras but the other day while dressing I reached for a bra and discovered the drawer empty except for my favorite Spanx and a dozen panties. After looking around most of the house I sat down on the sofa trying to remember where I had removed a bra. You probably guessed already; they were tucked into the end of the sofa cushions next to the used Kleenex.

Bus Stops and Diamond Rings

After my brother Mike died, my parents decided to send me to Salpointe Catholic High School. The emotional trauma for a fifteen year old was overwhelming. They must have noticed, despite their catastrophic loss, that I was depressed and needed the support of a religious community. Compared to Rincon, a public school, Salpointe had smaller classes taught by the nuns. Because we lived on the far eastside of town I had to commute by city bus. We lived on East 18th Street east of Craycroft in a lovely neighborhood. The bus I caught at the corner took me to Stone and Pennington in downtown Tucson where I would await my transfer bus to school.

On Pennington Avenue we would wait at least 20 minutes for our bus to arrive. On the corner of Stone and Pennington was a Walgreen's Drug Store. Extra pocket change would buy a bag of Sugar Babies or a Baby Ruth candy bar for morning class break. I always loved candy especially Baby Ruth candy bars with chocolate, peanuts and caramel. I don't remember ever buying an apple.

The afternoon bus home was met at the same location. I never had any leftover change so I spent time window shopping. My parents couldn't afford the clothes and jewelry on Pennington, the high end clothing district in Tucson.

In my senior year my mother took me into an expensive dress and coat shop called Switzer's. She bought me the most beautiful camelhair coat with a rolled lapel collar, raglan sleeves and a full skirt. Audrey Hepburn had one just like it. It was the style of the times. It was soft beige; I loved that coat. Mother and Dad must have saved for a long time to afford it. I don't know whatever happened to that coat but when I look at old pictures of me and my first husband all dressed and ready to drive off on our honeymoon I was holding the coat.

Ronel Jewelers was an elegant jewelry store on Pennington. Awaiting the arrival of my bus I would stand looking in the window dreaming of someday owning a little emerald cut white diamond, 1/3 of a caret, set in a yellow gold band with its diamond sparkling in its platinum setting. I dreamed for years of owning that beautiful little diamond. I never wanted a garish diamond, just my little emerald cut.

My first husband Ed gave me a little white gold ring with a tiny ¼ caret diamond engagement ring along with matching diamond studded wedding bands selected by his mother's jeweler, Mr. Meier, a private broker. In my second marriage we had matching plain gold bands because that's all we could afford. Years later he brought me a small ¼ caret marquis diamond. It was pretty, but not the little emerald cut diamond I dreamed of.

In September of 1997 Bill took me shopping for my engagement ring. After two or three jewelry stores, we finally found a store we liked. As we strolled around the store I came to a halt. There in the glass case staring up at me was a little emerald cut diamond ring in a yellow gold setting. Turns out it was a white diamond, the highest grade. Within the hour we walked out of the store and into the rest of our lives together with me sporting my emerald cut diamond ring. To this day I still find myself sitting in a room catching the overhead light in my diamond remembering how it took only forty-years to get here. Better late than never!

Coconut Crème Pie

Growing up I watched my mother make thousands of meals. I watched not cooked. She quite frankly didn't want me in the way. I did things like set the table, do the dishes and fetch. I fetched potatoes, milk, lettuce, flour, eggs and laundry soap (of course we didn't eat that), dishes and utensils, ad infinitum.

Because I learn well from observation, always have, watching my mother cook taught me how to brown a roast. The trick is to get your shortening (that's what they used back then) good and hot and then sear the roast on both sides until good and brown. Cover with a cup or so of water, cover with the lid of the cast iron Dutch oven and cook for several hours until fork tender. Great gravy comes from scraping all the bits of the roast on the bottom of the pan, the French call *fond,* along with the beef broth with which to deglaze the bottom allowing the bits to come loose. Ladle a cup of broth plus a little cool water into a jar, add the 2 or 3 tablespoons of flour and shake. (Do not add the flour by itself directly into the hot broth or you will end up with little globs of dough). Add the mixture to the pot of broth and stir until smooth. Great sauce!

Pies were her specialty. We almost always had dessert after dinner because not only did my dad want it but my mother and grandmother were determined to add weight to his post-war thin body. Unfortunately, after years of mother's desserts dad became very portly. Back to the pies. The secret of good pie crust is shortening and a good fork. She would work the shortening into the flour by pushing the fork through the shortening over and over until the dough looked like rice. Ice water was slowly added little by little until a dough was formed into a ball. Roll the ball out on a floured bread board and dust the top as you go so the rolling pen won't stick. A bread board, by the way, slips into a slit above a drawer in the wood cabinet. It was very handy on which to prepare pie crust or bread. First, fold the crust in half and lay it in the pie dish and then open it to avoid tearing. Crimp the edge using your fingers then add the filling. Mother's fillings were always homemade, "None of that boxed stuff!" she would say.

My personal favorite was coconut crème. Her creamy vanilla filling was laced with a handful of coconut; her meringue had coconut dusted across the top and as it baked the coconut would slightly brown. For me, Heaven would have coconut crème pies everywhere. Our family was comprised of Mother and Dad, Patti, Mike and me. That equals five pieces of a six piece pie. You can probably guess who got up early the next morning to eat the leftover pie in the refrigerator. Anyone who says you can't have pie for breakfast has never had it.

During post-war days we lived on a shoestring budget so the roast beef was very scarce until dad received meat cutting training on the G.I. Bill. He would bring home roasts, pork chops and ground beef whenever he was able. On the other days mom would cook low cost meals most families ate like chipped beef on toast, tuna casserole, macaroni and cheese and Spam with brown sugar and pineapple on the top. I wasn't big on Spam but I loved the pineapple and brown sugar which she also used in her pineapple upside down cakes minus the Spam.

Watching her prepare meals over the years I learned to be a pretty good cook myself. Cooking is just part of what I to do. Years after the war we moved to Tucson. Finances improved and Dad became a skilled accountant and started his own firm. This allowed mother to buy better quality food, nice table linen and dishes.

She taught me how to set a proper table: the salad fork on the outside of the dinner forks were placed on the left, knives on the right, blade facing the plate, followed by a teaspoon. The forks were placed on a folded real cloth napkin and the plate set two inches from the edge of the table. Where did they get these rules? I'll tell you where, Emily Post the Queen of Etiquette.

Mother's holiday tables were a creation of beauty. Out came her china, silver and Gorham crystal, linen table cloth and napkins. In the center of the table would be a crystal vase filled with seasonal flowers flanked by her crystal salt and pepper shakers.

Napkins were opened and placed in your lap. No one would so much as pick up a fork until mother did. The rest of the meal was history and so was all the food. Of course, the meal was always topped off with one of her signature pies. We soon started a tradition where each person got to pick a pie for the meal. When it was my turn you can probably guess my choice: Coconut crème pie with lightly browned coconut on top of the meringue. By now the family knew I got the leftover piece for breakfast the next morning.

Years later when I became a grandmother I was teaching our young granddaughter Logan about table etiquette. She would help me set a proper table. One of the funniest memories was when I said, "A lady always puts her napkin in her lap". As she reached for her napkin everyone at the table grabbed theirs at the same time. Where did they get their table manners? Obviously not in the book *Emily Post's Etiquette*. We all laughed but I know Mother would have thought, "Didn't they learn their table manners?" Her voice is alive and well in my head to this day. And, yes I have cloth napkins.

God Minutes and "A" Types

Many years ago while waiting for the doctor to return to the examining room, I looked at my open file folder. This was before computers were in every room. There at the top of the page underlined in red were the words, "nervous disposition."

Now I would like to think after thirty years of sobriety and "turning it over to God," I would have been converted from an "A" type personality to a "B" type personality, but it hasn't happened yet. Probably won't.

But the good news is the "turning it over" idea works. Before sobriety I used to make endless lists of things to do and I would run from room to room at home, or store to store in town and never get everything done. The mountain of tasks seemed limitless. Being stressed out was my M.O.

It was suggested I make a "things to do list" in order of importance and when completed scratch them off. I was only to focus on the task of the moment. The first time I tried this not only did I complete my list but there was time left over in my day. I call that "God minutes." God tucked in those extra minutes when I was not looking. I could never figure it out, but then why would I?

During my four years in the Barrio I was single and living on a tight budget. I was not poor by any means, but I had to depend on myself alone. I didn't have a credit card; everything was paid by cash. Like my parents and grandparents, if you couldn't afford it you didn't buy it. Then there are those surprise emergencies like a broken clutch in my old Geo, or, the installation of electrical voltage to my dryer.

Fortunately, because I managed fund accounts at the Tree Ring Lab at the University of Arizona, my checkbook was balanced to the penny each month. I paid my bills as they came in but there was very little left over. One month extra money appeared in my account. I rechecked my balance twice. Finally, I called a close friend and said, "I don't understand it, I have quite a lot more money in my account and I can't account for." Her answer, "Why do you question God's prosperity in your life?" I called this "God money." I never could figure it out so I quit trying. My mother sometimes called me "Little Miss Know It All," but this God stuff was beyond all reason.

These days at my age I decided I wouldn't worry about things I couldn't understand like God minutes, instead I'll just go down to the barn and brush the horse and give him a treat. That always chills me out. There's nothing more calming than the sound of a horse munching on hay. I suppose you could consider me a serene "A" personality if that's possible. Anyway, I'm not going to stress over that one either.

Asphalt Meditation

Three times a week I drive from Vail Arizona to Tucson to shop and meet with friends. During the thirty minute drive I have what I call, "Asphalt Meditation." Don't worry I'm wide awake. I have this conversation with God about a variety of subjects including music, the weather, my tire pressure, the hawk that often flies over my car as I enter the freeway from Wentworth Road, the green desert after a couple of monsoon rains and my late son Tommy.

The Red Tail Hawk has always been a sign from him that his spirit looks out for me. Sometimes when I have a dilemma, he appears. The hawk has been a spirit sign for me as long as I can remember. It often appears as a confirmation of something I am thinking about. There are times I don't know what to do about a situation and he will appear, then I know the solution is on its way. It never seems to fail.

My son has been gone two years and two months. The day I found out was a Saturday, not a cloud on the horizon. I had just had lunch with a couple of friends. I entered the house with two bags of groceries and was about to go get the rest when Bill said, "Wait, I have some bad news to share with you." I said, "What kind of bad news?" He said, "The worst kind. Tommy is dead." Did the world just crack in two? I thought he was going to say our granddaughter, but not my son. We only just reconciled after seventeen years. My response was, "What? No. That can't be." I don't remember Bill catching me as my knees buckled, but he did. The rest is history. The recovery has been gradual but gets better. Saturdays coming home from town after lunch with my friends is always hard. I dread coming in the back door but I know I must.

The asphalt meditation tries to prepare me for the inevitable; I will have flash backs. It causes me pain, depression and irritability but by the time I change clothes and come up to start writing again, it goes away for that day. Next Saturday, it will come again but I know now that I will continue to write my stories. They keep pouring out. I think my son still watches over me. I hope he has a few laughs and gets to know me a little better through my writing. There were so many absent years we didn't get a chance to fill in the blanks. I am so much more than he imagined. Through my writing I have discovered I am so much more than I think I am. My life has been pretty amazing and it's not over yet. I have no idea where all this writing is taking me but I am enjoying the hell out of the journey. As I have heard it said, "More will be revealed." Perhaps it will be on my way to town in "asphalt meditation."

My Orange House

I love our orange house. When someone is coming from town to our house my directions include not only how many houses from the corner it is but the color of our house itself. I'd say, "Look for the orange house with blue trim." They probably imagine the color of orange juice, poppies or worse yet, the color of pumpkins. Cinnamon Brandy is the actual name of the color I chose from Home Depot. To describe it is difficult because you would almost have to live in the southwest in order to visualize it.

In fact it is hard for me to describe. It is sort of terra cotta, but more like red orange, or maybe sort of the color of an orange Prickly Pear blossom, but then you would have to live in the desert to know that color unless you looked it up on the Internet. It sounds like it is as hard for me to describe as it is for people to visualize when I say, "I live in an orange house with blue trim." Maybe what I should say is, "Look for the house with the blue mail box with our name on it and a sorrel, a sort of orange, Tennessee Walker in the corral. He isn't the color of the house either."

Ramblings of a Looney

Lately, I have wanted to lose some weight; the plague of the post-menopausal woman. I wonder what I would look like ten pounds slimmer but I won't know unless I am ten pounds slimmer. Eating more vegetables is very boring but I can do it. I'd much rather eat French bread or ice cream (who wouldn't, mostly people who are ten pounds overweight.)

Loneliness: The other night I was feeling lonely so I called a friend to tell her. After hearing her rambling for forty-five minutes straight I finally waited until she took a breath and told her I needed to go to bed. Lesson learned: Don't call anyone about being lonely again. Maybe she was lonelier than I.

I love quail. I put a quail block in my garden because quail prefer eating on the ground. But now I get rabbits, ground squirrels and prairie dogs. The quail now fly up to the hanging bird feeder for the little birds.

I miss my little granddaughter. She is almost eleven and becoming too mature. She has a life of her own now (how dare her) and doesn't want me to visit her school classroom anymore. While she's getting older I'm just getting old.

Computer technicians. Ever notice when you call an outsourced computer technician you get someone with a thick foreign accent you can't understand. Now my computer is still broken but I am learning a new language.

My mother walked very fast and it was difficult keeping up with her. I wasn't sure whether I was just slow or she was trying to get away from me.

I'm a pretty good cook, at least my husband eats everything I prepare and seems to like it. The problem is I take an hour to make a dish and it's gone in 10 minutes while being entertained by gruesome T.V. news reports of death, destruction and abduction. Maybe I'll go back to TV dinners in the living room and watch reruns of "Grace and Frankie".

Nuclear Stress Test: They inject stuff in your veins that make you feel like you are running a marathon when the hardest exercise you perform is a walk to the barn. The test is stressful what with x-rays and scans that go on for hours. The doctor and I thought there might be something wrong with my heart. I was pretty stressed that I might need a procedure. Maybe with all my self-imposed stressing they should have scanned my brain instead.

Sauté pans: I invested over a hundred dollars in a sauté pan. I wanted to be able to flip eggs the way they do on the food shows. I've tried to flip eggs but they only stick to the pan. So I signed up for a two hundred dollar cooking class so I can learn to flip eggs. Problem is, I don't really like eggs.

My husband's office chair: My husband bought a leather office chair because he doesn't like vinyl. As time and wear have created holes in the leather he has covered them in duct tape. The problem is that now his chair is covered, you guessed it, in vinyl.

Bladder problems: I recently had a procedure performed to help my limited capacity to pee. Now I pee so much I have to wear panty liners.

I typed at least five hundred words today in editing my memoires. Memoires are pretty telling. I can see my family reading them and saying, "Who is she writing about?" Really, do we ever really know who someone is? We all have a secret life somewhere tucked away between the lines. Maybe I'll give them a good laugh. But, who cares I'll be dead.

The Titan II Missiles

After graduation from high school in 1961 my dad told me that Davis Month Air Force Base was installing the Titan II missiles around the Tucson area and were hiring. Dad said, "They are paying very good wages, why don't you apply?" So I did.

A Secret Clearance in the United States requires a thorough background check. Honestly, an eighteen year old hasn't lived enough life to create too much havoc unlike the youth of today. Anyway, I got my clearance and worked for statistical engineers whose job it was to project the man hours needed to complete the installation. Most of my typing was numerical but not always. Apparently they thought I was very good at what I did.

Memorable events come to mind in the course of my time there. One was the *Cuban Missile Crisis*. The base landing field was covered with fighter jets and other aircraft but what happened later was a big deal. I was returning from the second floor copy room when I looked out the window and saw a line of dignitary cars. The one in front had a flag with several stars on it. I was just about to step off the bottom of the stairs when a line of officers paraded by with a four star General leading the way. Apparently they were headed for an important high-level meeting concerning the Crisis. I had never seen a General up close. It was impressive!

Our building was a revamped barracks for the airman only. Of course the bathrooms were designed for men only. The women could use the stalls but the stand-up urinals were unsightly. The second memorable event during my stay was when the women working on the floor brought plants to sit in the stand-up urinals. It was very fitting that there were little flush handles dispensing water right into the plant pots. Women can turn any room from ugly to beautiful.

Roll Top Desk

My family lived next door to my grandparents in La Habra California during the late 1940's to early 50's. We had a small garage where the landlords of our little house stored some of their furniture. There were two items I liked best: One was an old Victrola crank handle record player along with 78 rpm vinyl records. I would wind the crank long enough for the record to play so that I could dance in the garage. The second was an old oak roll top desk which faced the window. There were several little drawers above the roll top when it was closed, but when it was open there were several little pigeon holes for letters and small items. At five years old, like many children, I liked to play make believe. I pretended the desk was my boat that took me on my make believe adventures. My favorite thing was to collect dead bugs who had fallen onto the window ledge. I used the little drawers to sort the bugs. One drawer was for flies, one for bees, one for wasps, one for moths and one for some strange winged specimen. Years later I wondered what the reaction was by the landlords when they finally settled in their new home and opened those little drawers.

Toby

Bill called our tabby cat Toby a five hundred pound lion because not only was he a great hunter he ruled the house. When Bill and I first married our home was on an acre of land with a house and a corral for our horses. The horses and the corral took up more than half of the property. Most horse owners would understand the unequal distribution of equine living space to humans.

One day I was looking out the living room window and saw something moving across the corral. At first I didn't recognize what it was until it got closer. It was Toby carrying a rabbit he had killed for his dinner. Funny thing is the rabbit was as big as Toby. It was hilarious seeing this cat holding his head as high as he could in order for the rabbit not to drag the ground.

Toby was always a generous cat and often left us thank you treats at the back door. You know, guts, tails and feet. He never left the skull. It always amazed me how he could crunch through the head and eat the critters he bagged bones and all.

When he was wandering the property he owned the place and took on his five hundred pound lion role. But when he came inside the house he became a sweet loveable "Kitty Boy". Lying on my chest at naptime helped me fall asleep. His purring worked every time. When I awakened he would have left on another adventure.

Toby was also a miracle cat. The month before Bill moved me from Tucson to Vail, Arizona, a rural community east of Tucson, Toby had disappeared. Bill thought maybe Toby had jumped into the horse trailer upon departure for a trail ride with friends. Somewhere between Vail and Sonoita Toby had jumped out.

In November 1997, Thanksgiving to be exact, Bill and his other horse friends brought their trailers to move me from my home in the Barrio Hollywood to my new home in Vail. That afternoon we heard a strange wailing in the yard. It was Toby, a bit underweight but insisting on a meal. I told Bill Toby knew his new mom was arriving and wanted to hurry home to greet me. We still don't know how Toby survived a month in the desert but that's why I called him the miracle cat.

Boulders

Life brings boulders; events that mow us down. They continue the older I get. I am a very tenacious person and eventually get back up and find something that brings me joy and purpose to my life. My husband Bill and I rode together for over thirteen years. But, there came a time when I had to hang up my spurs. An unscheduled dismount off my horse Apache at my age convinced me it was time. I grieved the loss of riding for two years. I also wondered if Bill and I would find something we would like to do together since riding was our passion.

That void was filled with Zumba dancing. I loved Zumba with all the wonderful Latin dances. After two and a half years my hip joints started rebelling so I had to walk away from that. I grieved that for at least a year. I couldn't imagine anything that would equal the joy my riding and dancing gave me. A close friend said, "I believe that God has something wonderful just around the corner, you just need to keep walking forward and it will appear." She was a very wise person because July 2012, my son and I were reunited after seventeen years apart. Yes, our reunion was better than all the riding and dancing I could handle. Now that he is gone, I have been searching and waiting for something else to fill the void his death created.

Writing has been an outlet that eats up the hours and allows me to tell a story. There are so many wonderful people in my life who have helped me grow into the woman I am today. The painful life events, and there are many more happy ones, have all contributed to my life. The author Richard Bach in his book *Illusions* wrote, "A problem comes with a gift in its hands." He also wrote, "You seek problems because you need their gifts." I don't always agree with the last statement, but do agree with the gift which appears after a painful problem. Bill, friends and family propped me up when my son died. I grew closer to all of them. I think too that I became a gentler person as a result.

Tommy's gift to me when he died was the ability to celebrate the rest of my life and to show others how to recover after the loss of a loved one and to celebrate the rest of their lives. My recovery uncovered a trait I was not aware I had, humor. Becoming a more humorous person gave me the ability to express myself in writing and to know that as long as I am still here, God isn't through with me yet.

A Fib

Atrial Fibrillation is an irregular heartbeat in one of the atrium of the heart. The rhythm is a combination of normal rate followed by a fast racing heartbeat along with warm pressure in the chest. Sometimes it returns to normal rhythm on its own and other times it requires medication or electrical shock. A Fib lasting too long causes the blood to start pooling in the atrium causing the blood to thicken. Eventually if not normalized it can cause a stroke.

My first episode was back in 2002. Bill was in Turlock California attending an early family Christmas reunion. I stayed home to barn sit the horses, dogs, and cat. I love our animals but travel is limited unless you can find an experienced horse person you trust to barn sit. I digress. I was riding my horse Apache in the round pen practicing some refinement I had recently learned in a Bryan Neubert horse clinic at J 6 Equestrian Center in Benson. Suddenly I felt like I was having a heart attack. I put my horse up and went inside to call a close friend who whisked me off to TMC Hospital.

After EKGs and medications to stabilize the heartbeat, they checked me in for overnight observation. Because the cause of the episode was unclear the Cardiac Physician wanted to perform an echo cardiogram that night. Meanwhile, I had to make a call to Bill I hated to make. After all, he was with his fifty or more relatives celebrating a week early Christmas. I struggled back and forth with it but finally placed the call.

Later that evening when the Cardiologist performed my Echo at bedside, a nurse laid a note on my tray. It read: "I'm on my way home. Love, Bill" I don't know why I questioned whether or not he would come. After all the man loves me. In looking back I can't imagine why I thought it an inconvenience for him to return home to see if I was out of the woods.

That event was a long time ago. My A Fib is fairly stabilized except when I drink too much caffeine. I love coffee. I adore coffee. Coffee is one of my favorite things. But if I overdo it, it triggers an episode. I have already given up alcohol, sweets, French bread, and pie (my other favorite things). Did I mention my mother was a fantastic pie maker? I am too. But give up coffee? It isn't fair.

Anyway, the coffee must be taken in moderation. Alcoholics like me are people of extremes. Moderation for most of us does not exist. We have to learn to practice moderation whether it is in food, exercise, reading, spending, art, writing or gambling. I love pie and coffee. Maybe someday I can have some pie but meanwhile I will have to be content with my one cup of coffee a day.

So far I have been writing in moderation. Maybe I'm learning. Although my walks in the desert have been replaced with my love of writing, I don't worry about it. I walk more than I realize because my steps are counted on my pedometer when I remember to carry it.

Experts say that moderate to strong exercisers walk ten thousand steps a day. So far I have only made it to five thousand. Now if I could only write ten thousand words a day. Whoops moderation Pam! There's hope for me yet. I know the walking is good for my heart, but writing is good for my soul.

Grief and Luggage

The thing about the loss of a child is that grief is overwhelmingly catastrophic. It doesn't end in a month, a year or a decade. Sometimes after several months, grief starts to lessen a little. But, just about the time you can look at his picture without bawling or hear a song and don't have to pull off the highway sobbing, out of the blue a familiar smell or song that reminds you of your child, and grief is back with a vengeance. Sometimes, it brings its luggage and stays for a few days.

Today a man I know shared about different types of prayers especially the Fox Hole prayer, "God help me." There are traditional prayers, for instance, the Our Father or the Serenity Prayer. But the prayer he shared about was when a man wounded in war calls out for his mother when he knows he is dying. A man in my grief group had been a Medic in the Korean War. There were so many men who died. What my friend remembers most were the men he was treating in the camps. He said, "They would beg me to save their lives." But, invariably, when they knew the end was near they would cry out for their mothers.

Tommy died of sudden cardiac arrest. I do not know whether he had a few moments before he died to call out for me. I hope he did The point is the thoughts of him dying in Africa so far from home I yearned to be able to have comforted him in his last moments. I began crying on Kolb Road by the Air Force base and sobbed the twenty-five miles home. It broke my heart to know that he was so far from home and family. He left this earth dining with strangers. What he left me was a broken heart.

The day he was born I cried with joy and deep emotion at the miracle I had experienced. Today I had flashbacks of his baby years, his toddler years, first day of school, graduation from high school, his career and the end of his journey here on earth. People say that when an adult is dying their life flashes in front of them. When my child died his life flashed in front of me. All I have left now are memories and a photo album. Sometimes when I am on Interstate 10, I listen to a radio station that plays some of his favorite songs. I can see him singing and dancing to the music. I miss his singing and dancing. God how I miss him.

Suicide

"Suicide is the act of intentionally causing one's own death. Risk factors include mental illness, depression, bipolar disorder, personality disorders, alcoholism, or drug abuse," the description I found in Wikipedia.

I never imagined I would get to the point in my life when I would think about suicide, but I did. The year was 1979 when my life had entered a black hole of despair. I was thirty-four years old, married with two pre-teenage sons. I had suffered from depression since I was about eighteen years old but didn't discover until many years later that it is a progressive disease untreated. I was sad all the time, I could hardly get out of bed, I couldn't concentrate or eat, and I had no energy and suffered from fatigue. The worst of it all was I felt worthless and hopeless.

My marriage was on the downhill, I was going to college, my sons were acting out defiantly and I had looked outside my marriage for love and attention. My business was failing, and my health was very poor. I had already discovered alcohol and pot as a way to ease the emotional pain of my downward spiral. Imagine drinking a depressant to treat depression; that is plain insanity!

That's the year I contemplated suicide. I would wake up in the morning praying to a God I didn't believe in anymore, "Please let it be different today." It never was. I had no means by which to make it better. One day after my husband went to work and the boys had gone to school I walked into my bedroom, into the dark walk-in closet, huddled back in the corner behind my long dresses in a fetal position rocking back and forth praying for the courage to drive off the Mt. Lemmon Highway.

It is hard to explain what happened next. Time stood still, there was sort of a large bright image of my sons finding my body at the bottom of the highway. The look on their faces was so excruciating I crawled out of the closet and dialed a hotline. I don't remember much after that except within the next week I was sitting in a counselor's office talking about why I thought I was so unhappy. I don't remember whether or not he/she asked me about my drinking. Probably not. In fact, I had no idea what an alcoholic was let alone think I was one.

My journey in and out of psychiatrist, psychologist, therapist and counselors' offices continued without any talk of alcohol or pot. This was so baffling to me years later how ignorant the medical profession was at that time, either that or I lied or was clueless. After all I didn't drink or smoke pot every day. I did, however, usually end up getting drunk when I drank and humiliate my husband and myself through my bad behavior when drunk.

Several years later a family member was sent to a treatment center for alcohol and drug abuse. The family members were encouraged to attend recovery meetings to learn more about alcoholism. So off I went hoping I could figure out how to help my family member. Through frequent attendance at meetings I heard people describe how they drank, what they did when they were drunk and how they felt about themselves. They were describing me. It was in those meetings I learned I was an alcoholic. I had a disease that had taken over my life. How could a nice middle class housewife, PTA, church going member be an alcoholic? I learned that people of any walk of life, whether from the park bench to Park Avenue could be an alcoholic.

Sobriety gave me a life. Yes, my first husband left me but my sons stayed. I now have thirty years of sobriety and a marriage to a good man who supports my recovery. I discovered I thought I drank because I had problems; but I had problems because I drank. It was the booze. I know who I am today, a sober woman and a useful women with tremendous gratitude for the people who saved my life. Today I have found a purpose to help others find a way out. If I had committed suicide, I would have killed the wrong woman.

Crossroads

I have no idea why I need to write about my first husband Ed. I have accidentally said his name two or three times lately instead of Bill's but caught myself. He created such pain and havoc in my life it was hard to think of anything good to say about him. Yet, the birth of our sons Tommy and Mike were his greatest gifts to me.

We saw each other not long ago, I think it was Easter. He was there with his wife, the woman he left me for. He looked heavy, bloated and red in the face. We had not had very much to say to each other since our son's death two years ago. I was never comfortable around him because his actions intimidated me.

Out of the blue he asked me, "How are you doing?" I wanted to say, "Compared to what?" But I didn't. I said, "Physically I felt good." He said, "What do you mean?" I said, "Emotionally I am still grieving the loss of our son." His reply was, "What's done is done. It's all in the past." My thoughts were "Maybe for you but my heart still has a large hole in it." I realized everyone grieves in his or her own way, I'm just relieved to know that I have felt every single tear, pain, shock, fatigue, lack of concentration, memory loss, depression and denial I have had. It is only because of experiencing all of it I am healing from something no parent should have to experience, except some of us do. My grief counselor told us to "lean into the pain because if you don't it only gets worse in time." I heard long ago, "What you resist persist."

A few friends of mine know my story and know I have been having some of those random thoughts that pop into your head when you least expect it. Now I'm not planning to contact Ed unless there is an overwhelming indication to do so. I can't see that happening.

I loved this man very much for many years that is why it is strange to say that somewhere deep inside me I still have a flicker of love for him. Probably because he is the father of my sons. Yet, I can hear one of the songs we both danced to decades ago in the 60's and feel a deep sadness. I remember some of our years of adventures, family vacations, the time we flew to San Francisco in our small aircraft, visits to Carlsbad California to see family and visits to Huntington Beach to see my lifelong best friend Joanne and her family.

We were married almost nineteen years. When he left it felt like my life was over. I cried all the time. If it weren't for my teenage sons, I would have probably ended it with a drive off the Mt. Lemmon Highway. God had another plan for me. Divorce is a death. The shock, anger, depression, weakness and denial seemed to go on forever. One day I woke up and the birds were singing. I hadn't noticed that for a long time. Little by little I started taking action to rebuild my new life.

I had earned my AA degree at Pima Community College with honors all the while working part-time to support my sons. I transferred to the University of Arizona and was in the middle of my junior year when life took another turn. I dropped out of school and went back to work fulltime. The struggles I went through as a result of the divorce taught me what I was made of. I discovered I was not only a survivor but a woman with purpose. I am not what I do but who I am. I am a smart, tenacious, funny, compassionate, kind, brave, talented, strong, spiritual woman. My life has purpose today. I am happily married to the man I love, mother of my son Mike and grandmother of Eric and Logan.

My life today is not anything like I thought it would be. I am privileged to support women going through the worst of times, and through my own experience, we find a way to live with dignity, grace and worth. I thought my life was over when Ed left but a new life had been given me. I found out what I was made of. An old friend of mine once said, "A warrior takes action despite shaky knees." We are warrior women and have climbed out of the darkest days of our lives into an existence we never imagined. Sometimes I think Ed did me a favor by leaving. I wouldn't be writing this story if he hadn't.

A Long Day

Thursdays are usually an easy trip to town, groceries, meeting with friends and gas. Today I had eight stops. One of them was to an Urologist. My prior urethral dilations were not successful so I decided to consult a new Urologist. A new doctor was recommended. His procedure is performed at a surgical outpatient facility. He also administers IV medication including Versed and fentanyl in a mild dose. This should help prevent extreme pain as I experienced before. He also uses a camera to see where he's going. God I hope so. I'm tired of getting up two or three times a night waiting to finish peeing only to wake up. Try to go back to sleep at 3:00 a.m. when the ideas for writing keep bombarding your head.

For some reason my intuition held me back from having the procedure done. I returned to my own woman Urologist who did not recommend the hospital procedure. The plan she outlined made more sense as we came to a mutual conclusion for my problem. I'm glad I trusted my intuition.

I'm so tired tonight I don't know if I can write much. Bill is getting some subs from Argenziano's our favorite Italian restaurant. I look forward to just kicking back and watching one of the two movies we received in the mail today from Netflix.

My costume of the evening is usually my muumuu or one of Bill's old, very old faded blue dress shirts. Bill is six foot three inches tall so you can imagine how long it is; it could double as a night shirt on my five foot five inch frame. Bill calls me his chin rest. When he stands behind me he can rest his chin on my head. One Halloween party we attended, prizes were awarded for the best original costume. "The Chin Rest" won.

Today was cloudy as we move into the monsoon season. It sprinkled most of the day but nothing measurable. The temperature never got above ninety-one degrees, but with the increased humidity in a typically dry climate, it feels hotter. What a relief from 109 degrees. Our forecast next week, a mild, cloudy 97-99 degrees with a chance of rain. I love the Sonoran Desert whether it's hot or cold.

The spring and summer explode into delicate shades of green. Cacti blossoms begin popping up; first the white tulip shaped Yucca blossoms followed by the Hedgehog. The Hedgehog has little cucumber shaped clusters adorned with shades of pink ranging from fuchsia, hot pink and a delicate cotton candy. The Prickly Pear and Cholla come next. Prickly Pear roses are usually yellow, but last year I discovered one with gorgeous deep orange blossoms. Cholla, the heavily thorn jumping cactus of the desert, is known for its ability to jump off the long spindly branches onto your arm or leg. Pulling them out you discover a barbed end that leaves a painful little calling card of unlethal poison that hurts for hours. They are to be avoided at all cost. Funny thing, their blossoms are some of the most gorgeous vivid colors in the desert; sort of a beauty and the beast combination. Colors range from watermelon red to burgundy and purple.

Desert flora is one of my photo passions other than our granddaughter Logan of course. Did I mention her Marana softball team won the Championship? Probably did. Serves mentioning again. Snapfish on-line processing does a beautiful job of enlarging my photos to eight by ten for framing. A local frame shop sells nice readymade frames and matts. A photo collection of my favorites hang in the corner of my living room.

I love making blank photo greeting cards. The Internet demonstrated how to make my own envelopes as well. For someone who forgets to buy Hallmark cards, my cards can be made for any occasion. If only I could remember to make several ahead. I'm always constructing one just before we leave for a birthday party or a funeral. It's progress not perfection! Perhaps printing them into five by sevens the recipient could frame them. Better yet, I could make my own photo gifts. What a brilliant idea! Isn't it interesting how writing takes on a life of its own?

I love getting handmade gifts. I still have a decorated apron, tea towel and recycle grocery bag from my granddaughter Logan that I whip out and hang in the kitchen where she can see them when she comes for a visit. When the family arrives for Sunday dinner I usually wear the butcher apron which reads in stenciled letters, "MIMI". Autographed in the top right corner is her name and date. The rest is decorated with flowers and stars. Someday I may frame it food stains and all.

I would imagine most grandmas today have refrigerator photo galleries of their families. I do. Framed in those little plastic see-through magnetic frames are the faces of history in the making. Logan's pictures change on a regular basis. Sporting her catcher's gear; grey pants, slate shirt #00 standing with her arms folded and sporting a scowl. The team decided by a unanimous vote to look like bad asses, which they are. The name of the team: "*Explosion!*" Appropriate indeed.

That's it for my photo story. I'd write something else but right now I need to call my sister Patti. Someday soon I hope to see her. Patti lives in the Baja of California, Mexico in a little adobe house with the Pacific Ocean as her backyard. Cobble stone streets lead from one street to another. The little barrio has two or three dozen adobe houses on cobblestones streets you wouldn't dare walk on with heels. You are headed for a sprained ankle, or worse yet, a fractured skull. I can't wait to photograph the Pacific Ocean.

Falling

Falling in love, falling out of love, falling down, and falling off a horse. I have experienced all the above. I have fallen in love, fallen in lust, fallen out of love when a marriage ended. I've certainly fallen off a horse several times and have lived to tell about it. But the falling down experience has been an age related event that snuck up on me. I turned around and tripped over a boulder in the patio I forgot was there. I fell down in the Oklahoma City airport as I came to the end of the moving walkway. I was looking out the huge windows admiring the Oklahoma landscape and tripped over my suitcase as I fell. Another fall occurred on the Granny Trail where I walk. One day after a rain I caught my toe in a soft spot and fell along with my Nordic poles. The Granny Trail is named in honor of my mother whose ashes are spread under an ocotillo cactus, her favorite.

One time while carrying a dish of grain to the horse, I caught my foot on the edge of the rubber matt, the grain flew, the horse spun and I took a dive out of the stall. Only problem is as the horse took off in fright, his hind hoof caught me in the leg and left a large hoof print shaped bruise. One summer I decided to buy a pair of rubber Crocs with the holes in them. As I stepped into the barn, I caught my toe on the step, flew up horizontally and came down on my head with a bounce. I remember calling for Bill. Problem is Bill has hearing loss and the house is a good two thirds of an acre from the barn. All I could do was lie there. Eventually, I got up and walked to the house.

A few days later I saw the doctor for my headaches. When I told her of my accident she immediately sent me for a head x-ray. The x-ray showed I had a subdural hematoma. The next day I was in the Neurosurgeon's office. Fortunately, the bleeding had stopped. It wasn't until about a week later an actress on a skiing trip had a similar accident and refused to see a doctor. She was dead within 24 hours. I could have died too, especially if I had been on aspirin therapy. Aspirin therapy increases your chances of serious bleeding especially if you are in an accident. I didn't die but I threw those stupid Crocs in the trash.

When leaving Ross' department store, I don't even like that store, I fell on a very small step from the sidewalk when I thought the surface was flat. Two women ran over to see if I was alright. I felt like such a fool laying there on the sidewalk looking up at strangers.

I saw the doctor thinking it might be a balance problem but instead it was a foot problem. Apparently as we age we don't lift our feet as high as we once did. The foot fall is all weird. For bruises, I learned a solution, it's called the R.I.C.E. procedure. Rest, ice, compression and elevation. Of course, by the time I walk from the desert trail or the barn to the house to get to the ice, gravity has already been dumping blood into the wound sight.

The color stages of bruising range from dark purple to an awful yellow green. What clothes do I wear to compliment the color of the bruises?

Let's face it, I'm not a gymnast or stunt woman. I prefer falling in love to falling down.

Jet Trails

Grief is like a close friend, I sometimes miss it when it takes a vacation. But like most friends it always comes back home. I know it sounds strange after all the gut wrenching pain I suffered for so long, but I got used to it. It was familiar, ever present.

I feel like I'm starting to forget Tommy now that it has been over two years. The grief counselor told me, "You won't ever forget him." I realized I'm afraid he has forgotten me. I used to get sign on a regular basis. It has been two or three weeks and I'm not aware of his presence.

I remember one time in particular when I didn't know if he was still present with me. When I mentioned this to my grief counselor she said, "Why don't you ask Tommy to give you a strong sign that you will recognize as a message from him." So I did.

While driving home after that prayer, I was on Kolb Road at the railroad bridge and I looked up to the southern sky like I usually do and there were two jet trails. That wasn't unusual because I have seen that every once in a while. As I turned heading East on I-10, there they were, two more jet trails. I thought it just a coincidence. I happened to look north just to prove it was a coincidence and there were two more. I turned onto Wentworth Road and pulled off the road because this was starting to send chills up my arm (a knock of the spirit Pete called it.) There in the western sky were two more jet trails. I started laughing, "Okay Tommy, I got your message!" It came across loud and clear.

Sometimes I don't recognize the way in which he lets me know he is present. I have been writing now since June sixth and much of my writing is about him. Maybe this is his way of communicating with me in a different way. Until I get another sign I will be satisfied with what is in front of me.

I've reached a blank out. Mostly reviewing and editing what I have written. I'm having trouble getting the "my book will be published someday" idea out of my head, yet Pete used to say, if you want something to manifest in your life picture in meditation of whatever you desire. Be sure to put yourself in the picture doing what you dream of doing. So I will.

Forgotten Grandmother

On Facebook today I saw that the new Marana Technical Elementary School had a public opening where my granddaughter Logan will be attending this fall. Logan was in one of the many pictures featured. Why weren't we invited? How would we have known there was an open house for the public? I feel so forgotten as Logan gets older because she doesn't want me to come to her classroom anymore. I get it, she is growing up, has lots of friends and doesn't want me there anymore. Her mother didn't call us either.

The longer time passes the more we are excluded from the family. Since Xander was born it is even more prevalent. I can understand the excitement of being a new grandmother; I am one. It breaks my heart to be less a part of her life.

Bill says he has no expectations of anyone that way he isn't disappointed. I have a real hard time with this. I have been a bigger part of her life up until this last year. Yes, we went to some of her softball games. We have gone to Marana for Easter, birthdays and the birth of Xander. But it still hurts so much to be left out of the family activities. I wish I could detach like Bill does, but that's just not me. I feel like it's another death. The death of the dream. I know, they are a family affected by difficulties too. Problems in the marriage develop and emotions run high. All I want is love and stability for Logan.

I'm sure they want to continue our "Going Back to School Lunch" and the money for school clothes we give them. Bill says, "You don't have to." Engineers are so cut and dry, black and white, no emotions. I don't want to be that way. Yes, I want to be included but I also don't want to go where I'm not wanted.

I didn't think I would hurt so much over this but I am. I can't deny the feelings they are telling me something. I set myself up by having expectations. I called Shirley, a close friend, who reminded me of the Serenity Prayer. I don't want to have to make an amends to my family. They may forgive but they won't forget if I say something hurtful. I would have to live with the guilt I would have created by opening my mouth. Accept the things I cannot change.

I love my family, I know they have their own lives to live. I can't afford to feel sorry for myself, after all I have set a foundation of love and joy in Logan's life. Just as I am facing a new episode in my life, so is she. Someday, I hope she reads my book and finds out I had a very adventuresome, accomplished and exciting life too. I love my granddaughter Logan. I know she will grow up to do something significant in her life. Because she is so intelligent, compassionate and kind she has the potential to change the world in whatever she is led to do.

Adventurous Girl

My earliest memories of my adventures started at age eight in Whittier California when I walked all the way home via the bus route because my third grade teacher humiliated me in front of the class for what she thought was my repeated talking in class. This time I was innocent but she blamed me anyway. I was to stand in front of the kindergarten class and tell them I was a baby.

I'd have no part of that! I waited until she returned to the class and took off down the hill toward the bus route, the only way I could find my way home. I sure wasn't going to go to kindergarten and humiliate myself.

After walking for over an hour I came home only to find the door locked. So I walked into my Aunt Dorothy's house where she and Mom were having coffee. The look on my mother's face spoke for itself. She said, "Pamela, (she called me that when she was upset) how did you get home?" As I conveyed the story to her I could see she was getting upset but it wasn't at me it was at the teacher.

Off we drove to the principal's office with my mother ready to blow a gasket over the incident. I don't remember much after that except I remember meeting another 3rd grade teacher whose class I attended until the end of the year. I would like to say that I quit talking in class but then I would be lying. I just made sure I didn't get caught.

Penn Park

Penn Park in Whittier California was my favorite park because it had enormous playground equipment (I was ten so it was all relevant), rolling hills, trickling water ponds, a bridge and lots of shade trees. The playground equipment included: tall slides, a tilting merry- go-round without the horses that you pushed with your feet and jumped onto grasping all the way. There was a piece of equipment with large rings attached to long metal chains on a May pole that went round and round when you grabbed hold and ran as fast as you could to get air born. The metal slides were very high and burnt your legs in the summer when after sliding about half way down you remembered it was too late to change your mind.

Joanne "Frone" and I loved the hills in the park because you could lie down and roll like logs. By the time you reached the bottom you were so dizzy you couldn't stand up. You could feed the gold fish in the pond your leftover sandwich crust and there were little bridges crossing the trickling streams along the shady walking paths.

One vacation summer day my twelve year old friend Joanne and I decided to ride our bikes to Penn Park several miles away. We didn't realize until we saw my frantic mother running down the hill that we had failed to tell her where we were going. Of course we didn't tell her because she would have said no. Unfortunately for us the fun exceeded our projected time limit before we were to return home from each other's houses. You know how this works. You each tell your mothers you are going to the other girl's house and then take off on your adventure. Usually you have a time you need to return home. That day we lost track of time and were now looking at my angry mother.

After a good chewing out she finally caught her extremely winded breath and said, "Those damn L & M's (a popular cigarette in the 50's), are about to kill me. Little did she know! Back then cigarettes were good for you. I think we got a week's restriction for our escapades but the most memorable thing was seeing my mom running down the hill gasping for air with that frantic look on her face. It's funny now but it wasn't for her.

The Corn Festival

La Habra California where my grandparents lived was only seven miles from my house. In August each year my best friend Joanne and I slept over for two nights so that we could go to the Corn Festival. It was awesome! My grandpa would save all his silver change in his shaving bag so we would have spending money. With our savings from babysitting and his contribution we felt rich.

My grandmother's contribution was her fantastic fried chicken, potato salad and boysenberry cobbler. Back then boysenberries were the preferred berry. When you went to Knott's Berry Farm, a family amusement park in Anaheim, you could buy boysenberry pie, ice cream, jam and ice cream topping. Her deep dish cobbler was to die for. As it baked the juices would bubble up in the corners and saturate the crust a little. This was my favorite part.

Grandma would serve us lunch as a midday break from the festival. The location of the park was only about a mile away. Little did she know all the food we had eaten before we got back to her house for lunch. There was cotton candy, caramel apples, and pieces of homemade cakes you could all buy for a dime. My favorite by far was the corn on the cob booth were you could roll your cob in a tray of warm melted butter. By the time we got back to their house we were stuffed but we ate her wonderful lunch because we didn't want to disappoint her.

The festival had attractions every fair or carnival has: merry go rounds, Ferris wheels, tilt-a-wheels and more. There were booths with ring toss, darts and balloons, fishing for prizes and a tank of water where you could dunk your teacher by throwing baseballs at a target.

We didn't want to go on the twirling rides until our lunch settled so we watched the western music performances of favorites like Spade Cooley and The Sons of the Pioneers who performed on top of a flatbed trailer. We spent our money on all our favorite booths of course, but our favorite was the "Dunk the Teacher" tank. We probably spent a dollar each, which in 1954 was big bucks, dunking our most disliked teacher in the school; but we did!

Of all our adventures as children, the Corn Festival in La Habra California will be the most remembered. Thank you Grandma and Grandpa Stowers, you made a difference.

Disneyland

The news that my family was moving to Tucson ruined my life. At least at fourteen it did. My friend Joanne was dating her future husband Gene and I was dating Roy. Friday nights at Disneyland back then was "Date Night". Gene was a member of the Coachmen, a custom auto club featuring customized hot rods with big engines for drag racing, spinner wheels and deluxe paint jobs. Friday and Saturday nights they loved to cruise down Whittier Boulevard looking for a drag race and showing off their rods. Gene had a 1950's circa Ford coup that looked so innocent but under the hood he had a high horsepower Cadillac engine. That night an impressive hot rod pulled alongside our car. The light turned green. All the other guy saw was dust and Gene's tail lights. Despite the show boating, the Coachmen had a code to help distressed motorist along the road. Primarily they loved to show off their hot rods.

Roy and I had the thrill of double dating that Friday night with Joanne and Gene. Disneyland at night was gorgeous with all the lights and music at the bandstand where we danced the night away. Back then you didn't have to buy the whole package deal, you could walk around and dance at the bandstand all night to closing. By then my parents allowed me to double date with couples because, after all, I was only fourteen. Fourteen! I still can't believe they let me date that young.

After the evening we headed back to a friend's house because her parents weren't home. We had what they called a "make out party". Everyone went to different rooms in the dark house and made out. It was that night that Roy and I really got carried away kissing and petting. We could have gone all the way but we stopped. He had the presence of mind to take me home before the inevitable happened. I was pretty naïve back then because our parents didn't give us the sex talk. Even in the 7th grade all the girls got was a menstruation animated slide show. Animation was less offensive in those times.

Today you can buy condoms at every corner store, restroom, movie theatre and restaurant. I remember giving my thirteen year old grandson the talk about protected sex. Boys at thirteen then were still obsessed with video games and sports. But today they can get a sex education what with all the commercials by Victoria Secret, the movies on Netflix, and videos on the Internet. My mother and father would roll over in their graves except they were cremated. Certainly my grandparents would roll over in their graves. I know because they were buried in a cemetery in Cushing Oklahoma. Families did not talk about sex, let alone exhibit provocative clothing or language. When I was growing up my grandfather always wore long sleeve shirts around us because he had a naked lady tattooed on his arm.

My adventures that last spring before we moved to Arizona were the best ever. My friends threw me a beach blanket party where you rarely went in the ocean you simply made out on your blanket. One of my friends, Shirley B., was a spoiled, beautiful girl who was engaged to a guy named Richard B. That day they had a big fight. She took off her ring and threw it in the sand. It was like finding a needle in a haystack but the ring was finally found.

Roy had a surprise for me too when he gave me a little chip of a diamond ring. For him the ring represented a commitment; for a fourteen year old a ring means you are going steady. But my mother didn't see it that way when I showed her. She chased Roy down the street with her broom screaming, "Over my dead body!" It's funny now but it wasn't then. Now both my worlds had fallen apart. I was moving away from my home and my boyfriend. Roy's father, being a wise adult, suggested we put my little chip of a diamond ring in the drawer until I was eighteen at which time we could decide if we still wanted to get married.

Finally the day came when the movers arrived. Joanne and I were convinced if we sat on the couch they wouldn't take it or the rest of the furniture. Needless to say the couch entered the van empty. How much power does a fourteen year old have? None, absolutely none! Isn't it interesting how our perspective changes the older we get? At fourteen I thought my life was over moving to the desert. At seventy-two I never want to leave Tucson.

After moving to Tucson, I did what every red blooded American teenage girl does; I found a boyfriend. When my California boyfriend Roy called I became distant. He knew something was wrong and it was. I had gotten a new boyfriend and that boy gave me a military high school ruby ring I wore over my aquamarine ring my parents gave me when I was sixteen. Of course in time I met someone else and gave him back his ring. Now my aquamarine ring is scratched but I have a new boyfriend. This one eventually became my husband and the father of our two sons. How goes the old saying, "You have to kiss a lot of frogs …."

The Catalina Island Folding Comb

"Twenty-six miles across the sea" is how the song goes. I was twelve years old when my grandmother and aunt took my sister Patti and me to Catalina Island. This was an adventure of a lifetime for kids. As we crossed the Pacific from the port of Los Angeles we encountered flying fish alongside the boat. The boat had a lower deck that seemed to just barely rise above the surface of the ocean. We could have reached out and touched the fish as they flew out of the water. On the upper deck was a snack bar where my Aunt Dorothy bought us snow cones and candy; the only time we ever got both at the same time.

We couldn't wait to explore the mysterious island. After Grandma's picnic lunch Patti and I rented some bikes and rode all over the island on little dirt trails. The island was a little paradise with trees and flowers and birds. Catalina Island had a quiet cove where we could swim and dive off a floating platform. Kids were laughing and splashing everywhere. Girls wore bathing caps the color of Easter eggs. The boys were splashing the girls with their cannonball jumps. All in all we had the best time. I never returned to

Catalina Island again, but I can still hear the laughter of my sister and the smell of the ocean.

Before we departed the Island my Aunt took us to a little gift shop where I spent my dollar on a little folding Catalina Island pocket comb for our little brother Mike who was letting his crew cut grow out into a flat top. He would put Butch Wax on the front of his hair and comb it straight up. He carried that comb with him everywhere.

Mike was six when we moved from Whittier California to Tucson Arizona. He was in first grade but wouldn't get to see second grade. You see Mike died on April 29, 1959 from measles complications. He had something called giant cell pneumonia. His death tore our family apart. I was fifteen and the eldest when I said goodbye to my childhood. I had to drive my mother to the department store to buy a white shirt and tie to dress Mike for his coffin. He didn't look like my brother. The way they positioned his head his chin was tucked in. His hair was combed to the side the way the mortician would prepare an old man. Mike would have wanted the flat top he had worked so hard to train.

I don't remember much about that night of the rosary at the funeral home. The lighting was low and sort of yellowish, the smell of the flowers especially the carnations was nauseating. My mother wore her pale blue shirtdress; I don't remember what dad wore except a face of devastating grief. He was an emotional wreck. The family remained in a little area behind a long curtain where we awaited the arrival of the priest who would conduct the rosary. Someone came back behind the curtain to tell me that a friend had arrived who wanted to see me. It was my best friend Joanne who with several neighbors had driven from Whittier to be with us. When I saw Joanne my knees buckled and I began sobbing.

I don't remember much until the next day when the funeral mass was held. The small white coffin was carried by some of the boys I knew from high school. It all seemed like a dream. Standing on the church steps I noticed the bright blue Arizona sky, the smell of the desert in spring, the sound of the cars passing and the birds singing. If I could just stare long enough I would wake up and everything would be as it was.

Mom and Dad were zombies wandering around the house after Mike died. Thank God for the food the neighbors brought in to sustain us the first few days. Dad just wasn't present, Mom tried to be the strong one, but this was her little seven year old boy. I knew something was very wrong when they decided to send Patti and me away for a couple of weeks to visit friends. Patti returned to Whittier, I rode to Hays Kansas with a family whose son I was dating.

Dad disappeared after Mike's death. We thought he might have had some kind of breakdown but years later we learned he would go to the cemetery and lie on Mike's grave and sob. My mother finally threatened divorce if he didn't come home and take care of the daughters who were still here. Although he returned home, he was never the same.

Months after Mike died we finally opened the door to his bedroom. His model airplanes hung from the ceiling by little white strings attached to thumb tacks; the blue walls looked like the sky. Mother and I sorted through his belongings: clothes, games, boxed model airplanes that would never hang from the ceiling, his mailbox bank where he saved his pennies, his shoes, Teddy Bear and favorite blanket. Lying in the top drawer of his little dresser next to his wallet and belt was the little folding Catalina Island comb never again to run through the flattop he had so earnestly trained.

    A year later my mom and dad painted Mike's room beige and turned it into a den where they would watch television, eat popcorn and remember Mike and where up on the ceiling one single model airplane hung from its string.

The Pacific

The beautiful blue Pacific Ocean. I grew up about fifteen miles away from it in Whittier California. If the smell of the ocean could be bottled, I would pay a thousand dollars for it. On my last trip to Laguna Beach, I stood on the sand on Alisso Beach taking in deep breaths of ocean air with the hope it would stay with me. It didn't. What I have are beautiful photographs and videos of the sound of the ocean. When I lived in New York the Atlantic was a grey green. I have a picture of the Pacific Ocean from Laguna Beach with at least four different shades of blue.

Sitting on a warm southern California beach with the sounds of surf crashing on the shore and the call of the sandpipers and seagulls is so relaxing. To return to the beaches of California would be so great if I could be dropped by helicopter, but the thought of driving on Interstate 5 and the horrendous traffic will keep me away. The last time I drove there it took me nine hours from door to door. There were eight lanes of creeping traffic. I thought my bladder would burst. When I saw the "Beach Cities" exit I felt such a sense of relief I stopped at the first fast food place I could find to use their bathroom and buy a cold drink. All those years of camping proved one thing; you should always have a pee pot for long trips.

I look forward to my trip to the Baja to see my sister Patti, but I have some anxiety about coming back across the border. The waits are very slow. You can get into Mexico but it's hard to get out. My sister hopes to get a fast pass to allow us to go through the fast lane otherwise the wait can be two to four hours. I don't think I will see myself whipping out a pee pot in Patti's neighbor's car. I have to be at the San Diego Airport two hours before my 4:40 p.m. flight home. Travel anymore has become such a hassle with the crowds, traffic, security demands and weather. Maybe I should have taken the bus.

I look forward to seeing my sister but not the travel. There are so many places I would love to see but Bill doesn't want to travel anymore. I would like to go to New Orleans and meet my friend Carol but she has not responded to my suggestion we go. Having her family there would make it really desirable for getting to know the city and to have a place to stay. I'll ask again someday. Right now the Baja is on my agenda two weeks from today.

Over the years Patti and I have had long periods of estrangement. She has pulled away from me because I wasn't able to do things she wanted me to do with our parents. She lived in California with our parents and I lived in Arizona with my family. When Mother came down with Alzheimer's we were brought back together again. Patti's religion and my recovery have made a difference in our relationship. She even came to stay with us a couple of days. A few years ago there were hard feelings because I didn't want to come to Mexico because of the cartel. She got angry about it. Time and age have changed both of us. I can only hope and pray we will have a good time together when I go. I also hope I have the energy to keep up with her. She will be seventy this fall. My little sister seventy years old? It's hard to believe we have grown so old. I wanted to go to see her in her home before one of us dies.

Her daughter Christine and her husband Mike will be in the Baja the same time I am there. They have a house up the hill from Patti. I haven't seen Christine since she lived in Anthem many years ago. That was the trip where I had an anxiety attack on the way home. Bill won't be going to the Baja with me. He wouldn't even if we didn't have our horse and cat. He is content with all he has experienced over his lifetime. He doesn't want to travel anymore. He is content to stay home. I on the other hand am not quite sure I have completely given up travel. My trip to the Baja is to celebrate the joy of being with my sister. She is the only sister I have who shares our same memories of childhood.

It requires a leap of faith whenever I do something that is new or frightening. It means I have to let go and let God again. All things are possible in this world. I want to expect good. Dipping my foot into the Pacific again is an experience I do not want to miss. Now if I could only figure out a way to bottle the smell and make it into a perfume.

El Pescador, Rosarito Beach, Baja, Mex.

I didn't know at the time, but in May 2016 I would make a reservation to go see my sister Patti eleven years after I traveled there to see my mother before she died in Rosarito Beach, Mexico. Plans were made, ticket purchased to San Diego and then Bill and I contracted some sort of strange virus. You know the kind when you feel sick for two or three days and then the fatigue stays around for three weeks. Needless to say, I had to cancel my flight.

I had to make that most difficult call to Patti to tell her I had to cancel. I was in tears about it. She said, "God must not want you to be here yet. It will happen when it is supposed to." I was guilty of expecting Patti to react like she used to and get mad, like Mom did and like I did when things didn't go my way. It was such a relief to hear the change in her reaction to life changes. I believe that her belief in her faith and her church community has made a difference. I know that my sobriety has made a difference in my attitude and how I react to change.

When August arrived I bought another ticket. Forget about Travelocity and American Airlines if you travel and have to reschedule your trip. All I got was a $50.00 credit from Travelocity and a $200.00 reschedule fee from American Airlines. Yes, I checked out the illness policy; it stinks too. My plane was delayed two and one half hours in Phoenix and a half hour in Tucson so instead of arriving at 10:30, I arrived a 1:30. Plans worked out because my sister and my reunion was more important than the delay.

When I arrived in San Diego on August 22nd, Patti and her neighbor Barbara arrived to drive me the one hour drive to El Pescador. This small community was once a little fishing village and is now a small residential community just south of Rosarito Beach, Baja, Mexico.

Seeing the Pacific Ocean again was a dream come true. My sister and I grew up in Southern California in Whittier not far from Huntington Beach where we spent many a summer day. Patti never wanted to leave the Pacific Coast, but I stayed in Arizona after moving here in 1958. Now I don't want to leave the desert I once hated as a teenager. Now that's a 180 degree change in attitude.

Located in the Sonoran Desert, Tucson is surrounded by four mountain ranges: The Catalinas, Santa Ritas, Rincons and Tucson mountains. Our home in Vail is 3,500 feet and looks out over the "Old Pueblo". The Pacific Ocean and the beaches of Southern California and the Baja, however, are my second favorite places in the world.

I arranged a four day stay, long enough for relatives. Besides, Patti has a very full life with her home, her Ultra Dry business cleaning rugs, her church and friends and her shopping in both Rosarito and across the border in San Diego.

I arrived at Patti's little brown adobe house with the blue wall. I was also greeted by her two dogs Azule and Playa. Playa was abandoned on the beach and found by my nephew Tim. Patti adopted her, of course. Patti was always bringing in strays. These are two of the sweetest dogs, but only if you are family or friend. If you are a stranger you are in trouble.

These two sweet dogs, however, turn into the neighborhood sentinels lying in the cross streets outside of Patti's house with a view of the stairs coming up from the beach. They lie waiting for a stranger to come unwelcomed into the neighborhood. You can hear a warning bark when this happens and one of the residents tells the intruder who has climbed up the many flagstone steps to the top of the street that, "This is a private barrio and you need to go back down the steps to the beach or we will call security." The dogs are the only ones that are allowed off leash because of their ability to protect the neighborhood.

With a nice cold drink in hand I settled onto the colorful patio facing the beautiful blue Pacific. Chairs were draped in bright colorful yellow, blue, purple and red striped zarapes, next to them a hand painted wooden loveseat surrounded by potted plants on little wrought iron shelves. As Patti and I sat and rocked in the chairs we watched a kite boarder zip across the ocean at twenty-five to thirty-five miles per hour only to discover later the man was at least sixty years old. I'm seventy-two but I don't think I will take up the sport.

Patti's daughter Christine and her husband Mike arrived to greet me. Christine is the daughter Patti gave up for adoption fifty-two years ago. We all sat on the patio admiring the beautiful sunny day. Mike and I walked down the flagstone steps to the beach so that I could put my feet in the ocean. Mike is a firefighter planning to retire in a year. To see Patti reunited with her daughter warmed my heart. I remember the day in the hospital when she didn't get to see her newborn child and how it broke her heart. We just never know what the future holds for any of us.

While I unpacked Patti prepared the most delicious dinner of meat, raisins and almond stuffed Pablano Chile Rellenos. Words can hardly describe the taste that hit my mouth when I tasted the first forkful. It was extraordinary. Patti has collected many recipes from restaurants where she and her late husband Lynn dined over the years. After dinner we reminisced until bedtime.

Tuesday was our trip to the famous Ensenada Fish Markets. The trip took about forty-five minutes with a view of the Pacific all the way. We ate fish tacos cooked right in front of us at a little mini cafe along the street. In addition to the crispy fried fish little dishes of shredded cabbage, pico de gallo, and guacamole sauce were on our table. There were also four bowls of questionable salsas ranging from mild to volcano hot habanero. I kept it simple with a little of the cabbage and in front of us. They were crispy, hot and delicious fish tacos. What a treat!

Next we entered the fish warehouse where dozens of vendors are selling fish caught that morning. Now that is fresh! In Tucson you never know how long the fish has been in transport. In the warehouse fishermen displayed perfectly arranged fish, some I recognized and some I didn't. We bought large shrimp and a piece of halibut filleted by the man who caught it.

On the table between us at dinner sat a plate covered with Panko coated shrimp sautéed in coconut oil. The following night the halibut filets were fried in butter with just salt and pepper. My job was to make the salad. Mornings Patti and I enjoyed coffee prepared in her Bodum French press followed by either cereal, fruit and milk or an English muffin with fruit and milk. The Jersey milk in Mexico is the best I have ever tasted, probably because of the high fat count. Of course only real Jersey cream was in our coffee.

Day three we packed a lunch and headed for Rosarito Beach. The beach below El Pescador was strewn with seaweed making it difficult to enjoy the ocean. With our umbrella, sunscreen and beach chairs in tow we set up our place next to a long pier. I headed for the shore in my rolled up capris. Patti calls them pedal pushers, a name for capris in the fifties. Rosarito Beach has several sets of soft smaller waves. I don't wear a swimsuit anymore so I never walked out too far because as one woman discovered the ocean is unpredictable and can spring a larger wave on you when your back is turned. She was drenched.

I took several pictures (Selfies) of me with the ocean behind in the background, proof that I was there. I always loved picnics on the beach as a reminder of our childhood days when the whole extended family would head to Huntington Beach for a day of fun in the sun. There would be fried chicken and boysenberry cobbler prepared by Grandma Stowers, deviled eggs, pickles and olives by Aunt Dorothy and Mom's famous potato salad. Of course there would have to be a cooler filled with soda pop for the kids and beer and little Vienna sausages and crackers for the adults. I never could develop a taste for Vienna sausages. My best friend Joanne would usually accompany us. With our money in tow we would head to the snack shack where little paper boxes of fried tortilla "Strips" with Catalina dressing for dipping sauce were served. Today there are hundreds of salsas but back then Catalina dressing was the best they could do.

Here's an amazing coincidence. My sister Patti introduced my best friend Joanne Pegler to her husband Tom in Rosarito Beach, Mexico over forty years ago. Of all the beaches up and down the coast of California to the Baja my only sister and my best friend were brought together at the beautiful soft sand beach in Rosarito. I believe that beach calls to us in a voice only we can understand. Great things happen there to the women who hear its call.

Ripley, Oklahoma

A few years ago I met a fellow Okie. I didn't know it at the time, but his voice always made me feel like I was home. Sure enough he was born in Oklahoma. I said, "I was born in Stillwater and so was my mom although she grew up in Ripley." His eyes widened, he said, "My mother grew up in Ripley." We discovered they had gone to the same high school.

I took on a project to learn more about my mother and her roots. She had kept her high school class portrait of twenty students. I composed a letter introducing myself as the daughter of Helen Elmore trying to locate someone who knew her. Letters went out to four of the people I found on the Internet still in Ripley or Stillwater.

One or two weeks later I arrived home to find two messages on my phone. One from a woman and one from a man. The woman was named Lela Shoup a ninety year old widow and a man named Wayne Snyder who turned out to be a cousin. Wayne had bought my great grandfather's farm, the same farm where my mom grew up. I made plans to go back to meet him.

After arriving in Oklahoma City, I rented a car so I could drive myself over the plains. I'd forgotten how flat the plains are except for the rolling hills. The mountains surrounding Tucson reach nine thousand feet. These little "rollies" the cowboys call them, look like anthills in comparison. I drove the hour to Stillwater and found my Grandma Elmore's house where in her late stage of Alzheimer's she pushed my grandfather down the stairs to his death. It was years later I learned about the aggressiveness of the patient especially in the afternoons. It is called "Sundowners". I found the house and remembered the chicken coop in the backyard and the little narrow garage where Grandpa kept his car.

The next day I left the hotel early after a scrumptious breakfast of biscuits and gravy with sausage. Biscuits and gravy are as much a staple in Oklahoma as refried beans are in Tucson. Ripley's business district was a little one street town. Back in the 30's and 40's it was a thriving community made up of ranchers and farmers. The downtown at one time had shops and stores, movie theater, churches, schools, fire department and a little town hall. All that remained the day I arrived were a few churches scattered here and there, a mini-market, the town hall, deputy's office and fire department. I walked into the mini-market to buy a snack and noticed in the back of the store there were a couple of tables where old men sat drinking coffee.

In Ripley, like any small town, everyone knows when a stranger comes to town. On my way to my car I heard a man call out my name. "Are you Pam Cunningham?" It was my cousin Wayne. Wayne's Oklahoma drawl was very thick. He gave me a tour of the small two room town hall which displayed on its walls photographs of historic buildings, the big fire back in the 20's that nearly wiped out the entire town, the construction of the Cimarron Bridge and the high school. There were photographs of school children in front of old buses. I found my mother standing in the middle of the children, her name listed on the bottom of the page.

Wayne took me on "Mr. Toad's Wild Ride" through the countryside. We saw herds of cows, oil wells and old farm houses. We pulled into the small cemetery where my Great Grandfather Elmore was buried along with his wife. Wayne then drove me to the farm where my mother had grown up. It was the quarter section my great grandfather homestead in the Land Rush. At the top of the hill stood an old Oak tree. The tree had grown up around a boulder. I sat under the shade of the tree and looked out over the horizon and knew at some point in time my mother sat under that same tree. I would imagine from that vantage point you could spot one of Oklahoma's many tornados on its path of destruction. I saw the old corner stone of mom's house, the cellar and the site of the cabin Great Grandpa Elmore built for the family after he homestead the property. I saw a corn grinding stone that Wayne had accidentally chipped with his tractor. I stood near those woods and tried to imagine the desire and courage it took to start a new life in the West. I can't even imagine the challenges that faced them. Breaking through the sod alone was a monumental feat.

One of the reasons I returned to Oklahoma aside from meeting Wayne was to visit where I was born, my first home and the Oklahoma State University campus where the night before I was born my mother attended a basketball game. When I contacted Lela Shoup she had encouraged me to come back at the time Ripley had its annual high school reunion and to attend Founder's Day. That night after the reunion potluck dinner there was a countdown for the alumni. By the way, these people know how to hold a potluck.

There was fried chicken, covered dishes of hot food by the dozens, salads, potatoes, rolls and more homemade pies than I had ever seen.

I awaited countdown for the class of 1936. There were a few still living. They called out 1936 and I stood and said, "I am here representing my mother, Helen Elmore Stowers." People clapped for me. After dinner this kind man approached me. He had worked the fields for my Grandpa Elmore. He told me that my grandpa was one of the nicest people he had ever known and one of the funniest. I showed him a picture I had of the farmhouse. He pointed to a little mudroom attachment and told me that was where he and grandpa had to remove their shoes before they could go into lunch. My grandma wouldn't have it any other way.

Saturday before heading to Ripley for Founder's Day, I stopped in the McDonald's to get a cup of coffee and biscuits and gravy. When I returned from the restroom I emptied my tray and left for Ripley. I looked in my purse for my wallet and it wasn't there. I poured over the car twice. No wallet. I drove back to Stillwater to the McDonald's to look through the trash. Long story short a young man and I riffled through the dumpster looking for my wallet to no avail. Needless to say my cousin loaned me money to get home. Fortunately, I filed a police report so that I could have some form of identification to board the plane. The car rental people were very nice. What an adventure it was on my trip to Oklahoma. I won't return again but I am so happy I returned this one last time to visit my beginnings.

Albert Einstein

While reading some of Albert Einstein's quotes, the one that caught my attention was: "The true sign of intelligence is not knowledge but imagination." Sometimes I think, "Do I have what it takes to write?" I don't have a degree in English, only some English courses in college. It's been a long time since I graduated, but even so, I do have a good imagination and a creative mind. Maybe that's all it takes to jump in with both feet; what do I have to lose except the regret that I didn't try. Besides, I'm not doing this for anyone but myself. Sure, who wouldn't want to publish a book but this is neither my expectation nor my purpose for writing.

Writing at this point in my life is an adventure more than anything else. I've been retired and married eighteen years now. My marriage and my sobriety are very fulfilling but something was missing in me. My desire to express myself in writing has brought me joy, pain, discovery and surprises. In the process of writing I become inspired with a thought which pops into my head. As I write the process takes on a life of its own.

For instance, in my piece about my trip to Catalina Island, the story of the folding comb I bought for my little brother took me to a painful place in time. It dug into my memory of the sights, smells, sounds, and pain I felt within the loss of my seven year old brother Michael. Sometimes my writing is humorous and sometimes it is very insightful. Thoughts sneak in I didn't plan. It is a journey of inspiration and fulfillment. I never know where I will start. I simply pray and ask God for direction in my writing, put my fingers on the keyboard and start typing.

I am certainly no Albert Einstein but I recognize truth. Richard Bach wrote, "Argue for your limitations and sure enough they are yours." One of my favorites comes from Henry Ford, "Whether a man says he can or he can't, either way he's right." Sometimes I have had to take a leap out of my comfort zone into the unknown and in doing so, I discover more of what I am made of. I am not afraid to step out of my comfort zone because experience has shown me that when I do so, something awesome happens; my level of self-confidence rises.

During the course of my first marriage my husband Ed and I decided to buy a Cessna four seat high wing airplane. The only way we could afford the payments was to make an agreement to lease it to the flight school. Ed wanted to be a licensed pilot and he became a pretty good one. Here was the dilemma: What if he should get sick or pass out? Would I know what to do? Of course not. So I enrolled in flight school despite my fear of landing the plane. My instructor was very experienced, after all he taught my husband to fly. I took that leap of faith out of my comfort zone, but if I am really honest, it was a matter of self-preservation not only for myself but for our two sons.

It turned out I really loved flying except for the landing. We practiced "touch and goes," approaching the runway touching down then taking flight again. I accomplished everything prior to my solo flight: Reading maps, using the radio, reading the instruments, plotting my course, checking weather, etc. The day finally came that I was to schedule my solo flight. My husband said, "I have some bad news. The flight school is going under and we have to sell the plane." I never got to solo but I knew how to fly a plane. What a glorious adventure. Whenever I hear a light plane overhead it immediately takes me back to my adventures in flying. I may not have soloed, but in the air, on the ground, and in my life my confidence took a quantum leap.

Ceramics Can Cause Divorce

I was employed by my family accounting firm in the early 70's after we returned to Tucson from New York. I was good at the work but working for my dad and husband wasn't fulfilling. The year was 1974 and I was at a turning point in my life. Living in the Hudson River Valley area of New York amidst artist, writers and educated people I was inspired by their talents and ideas. I took a ceramics course in Washingtonville New York, but moved back to Arizona before completing the class.

A ceramics class on 6th Avenue in Tucson was offered where I learned to "throw" on the potter's wheel. I loved it and continued to take the class. My ceramics instructor received a teaching opportunity at Pima Community College so I followed her there the next semester.

"You might as well sign up for an academic course in addition to my ceramics class," she said. I said, "I don't know, I was not an honor student in high school. What would I take?" "Why don't you enroll in Mr. Bustamante's Humanities course? I think you will like it." So, I enrolled in Humanities. By the end of the semester I fell in love with higher education. I earned an "A".

The 70's were times of great change with the Women's Movement. I was in college and, of course, was exposed to major social issues, personal growth and empowerment courses and assertiveness training for women. Additionally, I took several fine arts classes. The art classes certainly developed in me an appreciation for fine art, but I did not become an artist. I was pretty good at photography. My two courses in Louis Bernal's class at Pima College West Campus inspired me to see things from a different perspective through the lenses. Of course, today with digital cameras I can edit my photos on the camera, but with a film camera I was more selective about what I printed so I shot lots and lots of photographs.

After my second or third semester my husband Ed became increasingly irritated with my new found passion. He became threatened by my growth. I will never forget the day. I was excited about the Psychology course I was taking. After all, I helped put him through college, surely he could be happy and supportive of my education. That wasn't the case.

I remember the day my respect for him changed. He said, "I don't understand why I can't teach you everything you need to know." That was a major turning point in our marriage. Arguments were a daily occurrence. In March 1981 Ed left me after our nineteen year marriage and filed for divorce. He wanted to leave on my birthday March 1st, but he fell off a ladder and hurt his shoulder. Instead he left a few days later. The universe has a sense of humor.

By November 1981 I had re-entered Pima College to complete my last year before earning an Associate's Degree in May of 1982. I worked part-time at the college and at the University of Arizona test proctoring during the summer. I graduated with Honors in my Associate of Arts Degree and I am listed in *Who's Who in American Junior Colleges 1982.* Imagine that!

I owe a debt of gratitude to Carol Guerney Jacques for seeing in me what I could not yet see in myself. My adventure into the world of academia not only revealed that I was capable, but prepared me to continue further at the University of Arizona. Another quantum leap into seeing who I am and what I'm made of.

Achievements

Several years ago, ten to be exact, my therapist gave me a homework assignment. "List five of your greatest achievements," she said. In 2006 they were the following:

1. Giving birth to my two sons Tommy and Mike
2. Earning my college degree
3. Buying a house on my own
4. Starting a colt
5. Winning a lawsuit against Ed (my ex).

Next was a list of at least twenty other accomplishments:

1. Honor student Pima Community College 1982
2. Attended the University of Arizona
3. Getting sober (not by myself of course.) Sober thirty years at this writing
4. Dancing in a hospital benefit production
5. Finding my way to Jones beach (with two small boys.)
6. Making pottery
7. Studying photography
8. Cooking

9. I have a good eye for interior and exterior design

10. Earned four career promotions at the University of Arizona

11. Attended Alzheimer's support group for my mom

12. Let go of "my rights" when I was cut out of mom's will

13. Went to Mexico to see my sister Patti

14. Encouraged Jo M. to return to college and is now a retired tenured professor

15. Retired from U of A to follow the path with heart with horses

16. Met Bill Cunningham

17. Rode several large group trail rides

18. Learned to lope

19. Learned to fly a light plane and to windsurf

20. Program chair for a convention

21. Won a lawsuit against Valley National Bank (I was a whistle blower)

22. Owned a gift shop

23. Led a city petition to add Hearthstone Neighborhood Park and won
24. Started several recovery meetings
25. Learned computers
26. Sponsored several women
27. Made clothes for my sons and me
28. Cared for 24 horses at Milagro Stables
29. Took care of my parents when my brother died
30. Financially supported by sons after their father left
31. Learned several Country Western dances
32. Married Bill Cunningham
33. Discovered a cousin I knew nothing about
34. Went to New York twice to see Jo
35. Contacted Barbara Dabroski, an old friend from New York
36. Became grandmother to Logan and Eric
37. Diagnosed and treated for my depression and bipolar disorder
38. Went to Laguna Beach

39. Went to Arkansas and stayed with Joanne Pegler and Carol Fincher
40. Bought a Smart phone
41. Cook monthly dinners for our families
42. Reunited with Tommy after a seventeen year estrangement before he died
43. Convinced my sister Patti to come to Vail for a visit
44. Received successful therapy from Margaret Ed.D. for eight years
45. Landscaped yard
46. Walked the Granny Trail
47. Brought two women together in recovery
48. Cataract surgery
49. Yoga
50. Went to Stillwater Oklahoma to meet cousin Wayne Snyder
51. Zumba danced two years
52. Another trip to Arkansas to see Joanne
53. July 25, 2012 called Tommy first time
54. Redecorated living room

55. Went to Laguna Beach for last time

56. Began making cards and framed photographs

57. Writing my book

Hearthstone Park

Returning to Tucson after our four years in Rock Tavern New York, we bought a home in 1972 in Hearthstone, a subdivision on the east side of Tucson. The homes were built by a developer named Billy Jones. The home we bought was the model home meant to be owned by the builder but he changed his mind.

The house was a red adobe four bedroom with two baths, dining room, family room, eat-in kitchen and a sunken living room. It already had carpet and drapes because it was the model home. What I liked was the arch which led into an atrium in the entryway into the house. It was planted with bamboo, split leaf philodendron, a podocarpus and with a wrought iron gate. The large full length living room window overlooked the atrium where we could watch birds and butterflies visit.

One spring there was a tiny, well knitted hummingbird nest built in the podocarpus where two babies were tucked in like two peas in a pod. As the wind blew, the branch bounced up and down. The baby birds didn't seem to mind. The lasting memory of the hummingbird family in their new home paralleled our own.

Eventually, my two sons left the nest and flew away into their own lives like the little birds.

One of the reasons, aside from the fact that it was a great new home, was the fact that the builder assured the homeowners he was going to set aside ten acres for a neighborhood park. It never happened. Many of us were furious. We went to see Mr. Jones to plea our case but he was immovable.

In the course of the first few years in the neighborhood I had started a group of women who met once a month in one of our homes to host a "talented women's' coffee." We would each take turns hosting the group with a coffee and cake morning. One woman was a singer and pianist who entertained us. Another shared an interesting book she had read. One was an artist and one, a Japanese woman who showed us some of her artistic creations. But the star accomplishment of the morning was the sukiyaki lunch she prepared for us, floor cushions, low table, chop sticks and green tea. It was the hit of the group.

One month I brought up the fact that I was angry and disappointed that we weren't given our park as promised by Mr.

Jones. Many of the others were too. I suggested we carry petitions around the neighborhood and gather signatures to present to our councilman. After close to a thousand signatures, we carried the petition to the City Council meeting where our councilman made the motion to have the city set aside ten acres for a park along the Pantano Wash just south of Golf Links. It passed.

It took a year or two but eventually the park was cleared and a place was created with swings, slide, jungle gym and a bathroom and drinking fountain. Many trees were planted and before you knew it our children had a place to play together.

Today I stopped by the park to see how it had developed over the years. It had grown to 35 acres and was renamed Michael Perry Park in memory of the boy who had been molested and murdered by a pedophile many years before. Along with a friend he was abducted in downtown Tucson at a chess tournament. They were taken to the desert where one of the boys escaped but Michael was tied to a tree and stabbed to death. The killer was caught and sentenced to death.

It is interesting to look back at the history of the neighborhood and the park where so many children played including my own. Those were really good years when the children were young, innocent and filled with possibilities. I miss those days, those women friends, and my sons when they were young and filled with life, joy and possibilities. I lived in that house until 1988 and moved further west after my boys had graduated from high school and started their own lives and families.

Hearthstone Park and my women friends enriched my life. We all scattered to the wind as people often do. But for me, the initiative to take action to bring about change followed me throughout my life. There were many accomplishments to follow over the years and Hearthstone Park was only one of many.

Valley National Bank

In 1979 I worked for the bank in their Business Systems Department preparing payroll for several clients. I was a new employee to the banking establishment and did not yet know about bank politics or employee discrimination so it was no wonder that I was hurt by the seeming mistreatment I was receiving from my manager and staff.

I first noticed it when a woman teller had been transferred to our office when the boss gave her an attaché case, a phone and a calculator. All I got was a desk and my little plant. In order to talk to clients I had to go to another desk to use the phone. I did not receive an attaché case nor a calculator. It is pretty difficult to calculate payroll taxes on your fingers so I needed to use another employee's calculator when she wasn't using it.

It became increasingly more and more difficult to get my work done. On top of that, I had a much clearer grasp of how wages are taxed than most of the other staff members including my supervisor. They came to resent me because; First, I was not a bank employee. Second, I was knowledgeable in wage taxation. Most of what I knew about payroll came from working with my accountant dad. I was pretty naïve about politics on the job. Gradually, I was getting more and more behind and had to work more overtime to meet my deadlines. Not only that, I never took a lunch hour or coffee breaks because of the work load. My manager had little sympathy for me nor did she offer me help. It felt like they didn't want me there anymore when in fact they didn't. I was a threat to their incompetence.

Even though my clients were pleased with my work my manager put more and more work on me. Nothing hurts more than being treated with indifference. I felt unwanted and alone. I was becoming sick from the long hours and stress.

Finally, I told my manager I could no longer work there and that I wanted my back pay. She laughed at me and said to forget about it. I was angry and hurt that they didn't want me there. A friend of mine heard about my circumstances and suggested I look into the labor laws because something didn't seem right about it. As I researched I was directed to the Department of Wage and Hour in the Treasury Department. I wrote them a letter describing my dilemma. They asked me to meet them at the U of A Library to take my deposition. I learned it was a Federal Law to be paid overtime. I prepared a ledger of my hours and my reasons for leaving.

A year or two later while reading the local paper I saw a small column in the business section which read: "Valley Bank ordered to pay back wages to employees by the Treasury Department." My back overtime was only about $200.00 but every single Valley National Bank employee in the State of Arizona was paid back overtime including lost lunch hours and breaks. All those hateful women benefited from my whistle blowing and never knew I was the one who had filed the complaint. But I did. One person can make a difference and can reach back into their career tool box and take all their experience to the next job. Needless to say I learned a lesson or two about people. I'm not as naïve as I used to be, but most of all I learned one more time what I was made of. I'm a winner and a whistle blower and I'm proud of it.

Gifts by Nancy

The year was 1979, I had left my job at Valley National Bank without a plan. My husband was the accountant for a gift shop owner who wanted to sell her business. He thought it would be a good idea if we bought the shop and I manage it. The former owner took me on my first buying trip to the market houses in Los Angeles. The trip was fun and interesting but managing a shop without any experience of this type was overwhelming.

I was no slouch in the accounting area. Most of my working life I had the applied experience of my "office courses" in high school and my work experience after. What I lacked was the buying, pricing and selling of goods. Sure, the store had so many wonderful gifts. There were paintings and gorgeous stoneware pottery from Southern California made by a retired couple. Several styles of vases, china, Lucite bath accessories, gift cards, lamps, pillows, wonderful smelling soaps and hand creams, and dry flower arrangements. But, the items that caused the most laughter were the stuffed marionette dolls and the Horny Toads. One doll in particular looked like a saloon barmaid. She had red hair, black satin dress, fishnet stockings, earrings, and red lips. I sat her in a ladder back chair in the window. You had to see her to appreciate the details of her persona. There was no doubt she was a saloon bar maid. That doll brought a lot of curious shoppers into the store.

Horny Toads, a bean bag type of stuffed frog, were an original creation by the former owner. The toads came in various sizes from little ones that fit into the palm of your hand to one the size of a cookie jar. The toads looked very cute and innocent until you picked them up. There at the base of the belly between the hind legs standing at attention was a phallus, thus the word "Horny Toad." The look on the faces of little old ladies was priceless. It began with the look of shock and ended in embarrassed laughter. Despite the reaction, I sold more of these toads than any other item in the store.

After a year of buying, selling and handling the books for the shop, I was working longer and longer hours. Increased stress lead to failing health. I caught a severe case of Bronchitis and was in bed three weeks. If it wasn't for my one employee managing the store, I would have had to close the doors. When I finally recovered we put the store up for sale and sold it in a matter of weeks.

What I think I learned most from this experience is I am not cut out for gift shops. I worked several jobs after the store closed. I would have starved had I relied on real estate sales. I don't remember much after that year. I know that the winter of 1979 was when I contemplated suicide.

In 1980, Ed and I took what would be our last vacation together in an attempt to fix our marriage. I had no idea he had already met someone else. By March of 1981 he separated from me and moved in with her. That July he filed for divorce. I thought my life was over. I had never experienced so much pain in my life to this point. I wanted to die but I wanted more to live because my sons needed me. They were so hurt and angry at their father they didn't want to live with him. In hindsight he did me a favor. What seemed like the worst thing that ever happened to me turned out to be one of the best thing that happened to me.

I don't regret my gift shop, after all it was a lot of laughs, I met wonderful people and to this day there are things in my kitchen from the shop to remind me of another achievement.

So began the next chapter of my life. I heard it said, "Life is to be lived forward and understood backward." I understand. I am in a chapter of my life today I never imagined could be so good.

Windsurfing

Several months before I had gone through a long, drawn out, gut wrenching divorce a racquetball coach named Woody had befriended me. One day he asked me, "How would you like to learn to windsurf?" He and a few of his windsurfer friends practiced on Silverbell Lake in town. The lake was small but all you needed was a board, a sail, and some wind. I was hooked. I loved windsurfing because you have to focus on the moment. Pulling that sail up the first time, grabbing onto the boom and catching that first breeze sent me sliding across the lake. For an hour I felt total peace and freedom from the chaos going on in my life.

In July of 1981, four months after Ed left, I followed Woody and some friends to Apache Lake near Phoenix. I had borrowed my estranged husband's sports car because my little Toyota station wagon wouldn't have made the trip. That car was his pride and joy. Somewhere along the eleven mile dirt road to the lake I must have hit the oil pan on a rock. As the oil slowly poured out, I had no choice but to coast down the rest of the hill to the lake. When I arrived, Woody and his friends were on the lake windsurfing. I set up my tent and changed into my swim suit. Windsurfing on a big lake was a totally new experience for me. As I paddled out on the lake on Woody's board, I could look across the lake and see the ripples of wind on the water. I knew it was time. I stood up, reached for the boom and hoisted up the sail. When the wind took hold of my sail I flew across the water as if I were on glass. It was so beautiful, so quiet. I felt so free and happy. My friends on shore applauded me since I was the beginner in the group. Someone on the shore played a song by Christopher Cross called "Sailing."

The next morning I knew I had to call Ed. At that point of our separation he cared more for his car than he did for me. When he arrived later that day driving someone's truck, I was out on the lake windsurfing. One last dose of peace and courage before the crap hit the fan and it did!

Ed attached a haul line to his car behind the truck and I steered his car while he pulled me up the hill to Phoenix. We stayed at his brother's house that night after the car was dropped off for repair. I don't remember much after that. I suppose I drove his car home, but my head was still at the lake on the windsurf board sliding across the water.

Some months later I received a certification card which allowed me to windsurf at Mission Bay in San Diego. Oh my God, what a feeling! I was on ocean water within the bay, not on the open ocean. The waters are alive. It would heave and swell and send you flying across the water at much higher speeds than on the lake. I was squealing outload like a kid as I tacked back and forth for an hour or two. It was the most exciting thing I had ever experienced. I was thirty-seven years old but it wasn't until I was much older that I realized windsurfing gave me the freedom to be completely me. I couldn't see it at the time, but through the pains of the divorce to someone who didn't love me anymore, I found me and the freedom to live my life and to start over.

To this day when I hear "Sailing" it instantly takes me back to Apache Lake sailing the wind on the windsurf board to peace and freedom.

Barrio Hollywood

The house looked like one you would find in another part of the country. It was white with Dutch boy blue trim, pitched roof, step up covered porch and the most beautiful yard I had seen in many years. It was the kind of yard your Grandma might have. In the front yard roses greeted you at the corner of the chain link fenced next to a Mimosa Tree. The Mimosa has flowers that look like little pink fairy dusters. There were sweet peas, Hollyhocks, little orange and yellow trellis roses and, my personal favorite, the Queen's Wreath. The vine sports bright green heart shaped leaves and little strands of tiny bright pink bell shaped blossoms. On the porch sat a little pink bench and a large white ceramic "greeter" goose.

The former owner, Mr. Robles, had a sense of humor but most of all he had a green thumb. Don't even get me started on the backyard. There must have been at least three dozen trees, shrubs and various herbs (none of which I was familiar). I felt obliged to maintain the yard out of respect to the neighbors. They really liked Mr. Roble's yard. Because most of the neighbors were elderly

Hispanic widows, Mr. Robles was a very eligible widower who they liked even better than his yard.

This barrio is no different than many of the small old Mexican barrios of Tucson, but very different from my old neighborhood where most of the houses were partly surrounded by six foot high block walls. Many of the back yards in the barrio have smooth packed dirt with very little vegetation with the possible exception of trees. Then again, many others offered an array of flowers, well-groomed trees, shrubs and miniature concrete *capillas* where little statues of the Virgin of Guadalupe resides. Houses were palettes of every conceivable bright color. But, there were eye sores too. One yard, for example, had two rusty old cars, a refrigerator with the door hanging off the hinges and several broken bicycles strewn about the yard.

I lived in the Barrio Hollywood from November 20, 1993 to Thanksgiving 1997. After work the number three University/St. Mary's bus dropped me off each night at Columbia Street where I was greeted by the smell of green chiles and spicy meats on the grill.

One of my favorite eateries was the El Rio Bakery. They not only had every kind of cookie, donut, *empanada* and little cake you could find, there was delicious Mexican food to go. The very first time I saw my house, I had purchased one of their bean and cheese burritos. The beans are the creamiest (probably prepared with lard), but the combination of the melted cheese and hot beans can stick to the roof of your mouth and burn like hell. But one bite of the glazed donuts was pure heaven.

Many mornings I left for the bus a little early so I could get to the bakery just as the baker was frying the donuts in his little rolling deep fryer. I couldn't just buy one, I usually bought three. Six months and ten pounds heavier, I had to give up my morning visits to the bakery. Why can't broccoli be fattening and donuts be good for you?

The sounds of the barrio are alive with barking dogs, children, music and the bells of the familiar *paleta* cart. Paletas are delicious frozen fresh fruit juice bars sold by little carts pushed by street vendors. The carts have a strand of apple sized bells with the most melodious sound I can never quite describe. One time I made the mistake of buying my dogs Cayce and Geno a coconut *coco* paleta. After that whenever the vendor's bells would ring, the dogs would run in circles and salivate; I would too.

The neighbors, *vecinos* are friendly and welcoming. Although I learned many names and phrases in Spanish the neighbors politely smiled at me and my attempts at conversation. I think they appreciated me trying. Little by little I learned enough to greet people, ask for food, inquire about the weather, ask about their families, and for directions. What more is there?

The history in that barrio goes back four generations. I met an 80 year old man whose grandparents lived in the house in which he resided. He told me, "When I was a little boy, I used to swim in the Santa Cruz River." Rivers in Arizona are large dry washes which only run when the monsoon rains come. Back one hundred years ago there were Mesquite Trees along the banks and people boated and fished. Many of the residents in the barrio were third or fourth generation. It is not unusual to see three generations all living together. For instance, my next door neighbor lived in the original little two bedroom adobe. When their children grew up and got married, they would build an addition. When the grandchildren grew up and got married they would add another. Although the properties were fairly narrow, they were very deep. Large enough to stable a horse. Actually, there was a neighbor who did just that. Apparently the laws respecting horses were grandfathered in as new property laws were written.

The neighborhood was fairly self-supporting surrounded by little markets called *tienditas*, bakeries, meat markets, tortilla factories, restaurants, beauty salons and barbers. And of course the local Catholic Church where little old Mexican women wearing hats and carrying their purses tucked under their arms would toddle off at 6:30 a.m. to early morning mass. You had to respect their dedication even if you weren't Catholic.

Friday nights were always exciting. By midnight you were usually awakened by gunshots. On holidays the music, laughter and comradery were boisterous. Being awakened at 2:00 a.m. by guitar strumming *mariachis* was not one of them. Mother's and Father's Days are very important consequently children would pay to have their parents serenaded at their bedroom windows with little *mananitas* a traditions I eventually came to appreciate.

My four years in the Barrio Hollywood was a cultural education. There lies history in families, art, education, and tradition.

It was a joy and a privilege to have lived there four short years. The memories live on.

If you ride it, it will come

My friends tell me I should write this story. The year was 1995. A book called *Passages* encouraged its readers, especially those in their 50's, to follow up on some unfinished childhood passions. Passions started in childhood but like many of us, had been put on the shelf as adulthood crept in. One dream was dancing, but the other was my love of horseback riding. So, at fifty-one, I signed up for some dance lessons and English riding lessons. After six months of "developing a good seat", I was attracted to western trail riding.

My first western riding instructor Tracy was a barrel racer, but not really a trainer. After she left town I was led to Barbara, a woman whose flyer appeared on my windshield at a local Country Western saloon where I was taking dance lessons. (Remember my other dream?) "Five lessons for the price of four", she advertised. I saw this as a sign and made an appointment.

The day I arrived, my instructor had the horse already saddled up and ready to ride. I got on, rode around the round pen for an hour and got off. Now she was very helpful, but I wanted more so I told her "I want to be more than a passenger, I want to learn everything from the ground up." She was elated and said, "Great! I was hoping you would say that." That started my schooling in a way of handling horses I never imagined possible. Needless to say, I was hooked. I showed up every week, sometimes twice a week for the next year. I did everything I could to help her just to hang around her to learn. I cleaned stalls, tack, brought her horses from the barn, you name it.

A year later, I decided to leave my eleven-year desk job at the university to follow my heart. Above my desk I had a sign that read: "If you ride it, it will come." A horse, of course! I borrowed the phrase from the "Field of Dreams" movie. I believed that somehow, some way, God would bring a horse into my life and I didn't have to figure out how. After eleven years, I retired and started looking for a job related to horses. I took little flyers to every feed store, Western wear store, tack store and stable I could find. I talked to everyone I knew about my dream. Many of them thought I was nuts, but I knew something they apparently didn't know. If you follow the path with heart, God will do the rest. Of course you have to do the footwork.

One day at my trainer's barn, her farrier told me about a barn assistant job and gave me an address. I called and set an appointment for Saturday. The next day, a woman in a tack store gave me another lead, I called and set an appointment for Sunday. Saturday arrived and I met the farrier to drive to the job interview. As we drove the many streets to the stable, the street names started sounding familiar, you know, like Déjà vu? As we turned on Milagro Street (which means miracle) I said, "You won't believe this", this is where I'm supposed to be tomorrow too. He looked on the page of my planner to see the same name and address; sure enough it was the same job. Coincidence? He said, "I think you're meant to have this job." Of course I got it and loved it. I took care of twenty to twenty-four horses, cleaned stalls, fed, turned them out, barn sat, and got many opportunities to ride others' horses. It was great. The horses taught me so much.

Then it happened. One Saturday in June, my trainer and I went to a cow working clinic in Benson Arizona and during the lunch break; a man had stolen my chair. His name was Bill. Several of us visited but he and I really hit it off. Come to find out, he liked to start colts, lead trail rides, and knew many horse people. I said, "Would you mind taking my business card, I'm looking for work with horses. If you know of anyone who needs someone like me, I'd appreciate a call." A week went by, no call. Finally, the following week I got a call from Bill. He said, "I couldn't find you any work, but would you like to go to dinner Saturday night?"

Now I have to tell you I wasn't looking for a man. I was really more interested in finding a horse, but he was a pleasant sort of fella who certainly rode well, had good sense of humor and could dance too. So I said yes. That fella kept me busy every Saturday night after that. Problem is he stole my heart. Six months later he stole my name. December 14, 1997 we were married in our patio with all our horse friends. I even got to ride in a horse drawn carriage. Every woman's dream, a one-woman parade!

Now here's the part I could not have planned. Remember my slogan: "If you ride it, it will come?" Well right there at the wedding, in front of all our friends, he gave me his favorite quarter horse Dandy as a wedding gift. I nearly fainted. As I looked around the room through tear-drenched eyes, my trainer's tear filled eyes met mine. She knew about my dream and my theme. In fact, there wasn't a dry eye in the place.

I truly believed a horse would come into my life, I just didn't know he would have a man attached to it.

The Ride for My Life

For the next two years I rode as often as I could and attended horsemanship clinics. Things were going pretty well until one summer night in 1998.

My husband and I had gone out for a short ride at sunset. I was riding a horse Bill had been training when on our way home Bill rode out of sight for a moment. As my young three-year-old colt bolted to catch up with my husband's horse we rounded a mesquite tree, I lost my left stirrup, my center in the saddle, rolled off and bounced on my back landing with my head in the base of a Yucca. I knew I was hurt but just didn't know how seriously. My husband made sure my vital signs were okay before riding off to a neighboring house to call for help. By then it was dark and I'm lying on the desert floor looking up at the stars thinking, "God, this looks like a good night to die." This thought was replaced by the thoughts of scorpions, snakes or spiders showing up for a visit. I was terrified. Fortunately for me they had business elsewhere. Within 45 minutes the paramedics and a helicopter arrived to assist in my rescue. For the first time in my life I received an unscheduled helicopter ride.

I didn't know until the next day whether or not I would walk again. The Doctor told me I had three compression fractures in my vertebrae. Gratefully I was able to walk but the road back to recovery was a long and painful one. I didn't know if I would ever ride a horse again so I decided during the eight weeks of my recovery and physical therapy I would visualize myself riding my horse. I would not entertain the idea of not riding my horse again. After all I'd waited all my life for a horse. It wasn't his fault I came off his back. I believed deep inside I would ride again despite the pain.

At eight weeks of recovery my husband steadied my horse while I mounted him from the panel. I was so scared my heart was pounding, I felt like I would lose my lunch, and my palms were sweating. But I did it! Bill led me in a wide circle once. It was hard, but I knew then that I would ride again and I did for thirteen more years.

Apache

My beautiful Dandy, Bill's wedding gift to me was a fine horse except he had advanced navicular in his right front leg. After what seemed like months of trying to rehabilitate my lame horse, I decided to buy another in June. After several weeks of looking at some nice horses I couldn't find one. I was beginning to wonder if I would.

One Tuesday morning after breakfast, I was reading the "classified horse ads" and saw one. It read, "Registered paint quarter horse buckskin." Being pretty new at the horse industry, I called to ask about him. Well the owner described everything about him and come to find out he was a "breeding stock" paint and had no spots. He was what she called a gruella buckskin and insisted, "I had to see him." He belonged to her son. So I made an appointment to come by about 8:30 a.m. The name of the ranch sounded vaguely familiar. On the way to the ranch, I said a little prayer: "God, I haven't had much luck finding a horse. If I'm meant to have this one, please give me a sign.

When I arrived at 8:30 a.m., it was Deja vu. I knew the name of the ranch sounded familiar. I had been there several years before with my golden retriever for obedience training. (Sign #1) As I strolled the grounds looking for the young man I was to meet, (it was his horse), and his mother greeted me. "My son will be back from his ride on the horse any minute. He doesn't know you are coming because you called after he had left." Suddenly the young man and his girlfriend rode up. As they dismounted, his mother introduced us.

"Ben," she said, "this is Pam Cunningham, she's come to look at Apache." His eyes got very big as he and his girlfriend's mouths flew open. They said, "God, we just met a woman on the trail named Sandy who said she had a friend looking for a trail horse and could she give her my phone number; her name is Pam Cunningham.

Boy, talk about a coincidence!" (Sign #2)

Needless to say, I fell in love with Apache. Not only was he beautiful but we connected. He had these "angel eyes." (Sign #3) I called Bill from the tack room describing everything about him. Bill said, "Sounds like you found your horse."

When I got home there was a message from Sandy on my phone. "There's a young man in my neighborhood who has a really nice buckskin for sale; here's his number." I phoned Sandy and told her my story. We laughed at the unusual circumstances (signs) and the interesting events that were born from my prayer. Coincidence? We didn't think so.

The Desert Speaks

We loved to go trail riding in the beautiful Sonoran Desert. In fact, you could find us out just about every morning on our horses headed up one of the many washes or *arroyos*. Sometimes we could be found bushwhacking on horseback, one of our favorite things to do. Needless to say, bushwhacking in the Arizona desert is very challenging. There is a prickly cactus awaiting you at every turn. It does make you and your horse pay close attention.

One of the reasons we like to ride the washes is because we get to see wildlife that one does not normally see from the road. There are javelina, jack rabbits, coyotes, hawks, vultures, Great Horned owl, quail, dove, cactus wren, and snakes to mention a few. Because we ride so early in the morning, we often see deer as well. But, once in a while you spot something you aren't quite prepared for.

One Sunday morning, Bill and I were headed east in the wash. It was a beautiful sunny fall day typical of the Arizona desert. Our horses are used to wildlife and the noises of the desert, so they are pretty calm. Once in a while a covey of quail will scatter out from under some prickly pear cactus creating quite a clatter of wings. Now this can spook most horses, but ours are used to it. On this particular Sunday, however, we decided to take a different fork in the wash from our normal one. I was leading on my buckskin Apache when we suddenly came to a stop. Apache's ears were forward signaling he had spotted something. I just knew it was those javelina we normally see. But boy was I in for a surprise.

There in the wash still dressed in his feet pajamas sat a little two year old boy calling for his mommy. His name was Jason. We couldn't believe it at first, that's not something you see every day. But there he was. Apache lowered his head to check out this curious little human being. I dismounted to pick up the little boy and to make sure he wasn't hurt. Aside from being lost and afraid, he wasn't hurt. I noticed that he was looking at my horse Apache the way little ones do when they see something new.

Bill and I looked around but could see no house close by. I picked up the little boy and assured him that we would find his mommy but we had to get up on the horses. He didn't seem to be afraid when I let him pat Apache on the face. Horses are so great with small children, they seem to intuitively know to me gentle. I handed the little boy up to Bill to carry on his horse. Then we faced the decision of whether to go back home and call the Sheriff's Department or to look for a house in the area. Something told me that we should head south in the wash for a while. Sure enough in about 10 minutes, we found a house. As we approached it we noticed that the little boy had stopped crying and had a look of excitement on his face. Do you suppose in all that desert and that big wash we had actually found his home?

As we approached the house we started yelling for someone. By now, I was ponying Bill's other horse since he was carrying the boy in front of him. No one answered. At the same time Bill dismounted and as he carried the little boy up to the house a man was coming out. When he saw the little boy his face lit up as bright as a Christmas tree. "Jason, am I glad to see you. Your mommy and daddy have been looking for you for over an hour." It seems that little Jason, almost a year and a half old, had wandered out of the house while mommy and daddy were still sleeping because he wanted to go to Grandpa's house. Funny thing about it, Jason wanted to sit back on top of that big horse more than he wanted to go to Grandpa. It took a little coaxing, but he finally went to him.

As Bill and I rode home, we thought about all the wildlife we often see in the wash and what could have happened to that little boy. I guess we were lucky we were in the right place at the right time to find this little one out on a journey of his own. It's funny how things work out. We were really fortunate to have been a part of Jason's journey that morning.

Sign

When driving I notice a stop, curve in the road sign, or an equestrian trail sign. These signs warn me to pay attention. Sign of the physic nature asks me to pay attention as well. We all have sign that points us in the right direction. For example, an intuitive feeling that tells us to cross the street when we see someone coming but don't know why we crossed the street. A hawk that flies over your car or your head when you are thinking about a problem and the solution suddenly pops into your mind with an answer you haven't thought of before. For me it is a confirmation of the path to follow. It never fails.

I remember Pete telling me I would recognize sign when I saw or felt it. My second marriage was deteriorating to the point of no return. All attempts by me to "fix" it failed. The person I needed to fix was me. Through years of recovery and meditation I learned to recognize sign. I often walked my dog in the morning before I started my work day. One morning a sign appeared. I was walking across Country Club south of Broadway in a very old neighborhood I saw not one but three hawks sitting on the phone line. My thought just before it was whether I should ask for a divorce. I had postponed it for about three years. Not only had I received not one but three signs. The hawks confirmed the question I asked. In looking back I know it was the right decision.

This meant we would have to sell the house and move. Because we didn't want to split our two dogs up we agreed that whoever found a house with a yard first kept the dogs. The dogs loved the yard in my new house.

But, before I would come to enjoy the house I first had to find it. After two months of looking at several neighborhoods within three miles of the University of Arizona I had come up empty. Some were too expensive, some in condition beyond my knowledge of repair and some in barrios owned by families whose grandparents had owned the home. They were there for life.

One evening at sunset I was sitting at the top of "A" Mountain trying to visualize an area I might have missed. There in the western sky was a hawk in front of a blazing orange sunset. That was sign. "Okay, I'll take another look again." I got out of the car and happened to look north. I could see the Deaf and Blind school on

Speedway but just south of it the street lights came on. I couldn't remember driving through that area. Because it was dark by the time I got down the mountain I decided to go back the next day.

Sure enough, I had not driven this neighborhood. I drove up and down one street after another but couldn't see a for sale sign. I was about to leave when I came to Ontario St. Do I turn left or right? My gut told me to turn right back toward the Interstate where I would return home. There, three houses down on the right was a for sale sign in front of a little white house with Dutch boy blue trim. As I walked the property I entered the gate to the backyard. Had I entered another world? The shaded yard was filled with beautiful trees and shrubs. As I stood in awe I knew the house would be mine. The house was as I saw it in my meditation. Pete would say, "Put yourself in the picture." It was perfect. Thirty days later the house was mine.

Sign can come as a physical feeling. It could be something someone shared in a group that makes the hairs on my arm stand up. I could be watching a movie and hear something that would trigger a long forgotten memory. It could an answer in a dream. Upon awakening you suddenly know what to do.

Several years passed after my divorce. My life got real busy with work, friends, and fun. But as I mentioned before, I had met Bill in the horse community. One afternoon he asked me if he could cook me dinner. I accepted. After dinner he walked down to saddle one of his horses so that I could ride around the corral. As I stood on the front porch watching him saddle the horse the hairs on my left arm stood up. I remember thinking, "Is this the man I will marry?" As much as I tried to dismiss this thought, sign never lies. In meditation the man wore a blue shirt, white cowboy hat, and led his horse on a rope halter. The corral was in the front of the house, instead of behind. We could look out the big picture window and watch the horses. This was exactly as I had seen it in meditation.

In six months we were married in our patio under the mesquite trees with all our friends in western attire. A horse drawn carriage drove me down the road in my one woman parade. Bill and I have been married eighteen years and remain best friends and sweethearts. We support each other in and through everything life hands us.

Sign has never lied. It sometimes answers questions that have not yet been asked. How does that happen? After my son Tommy died the hawks were around most of the time. On the day my family held our memorial service for him a hawk flew over us. My spirit hawk appears when I need that reassurance I am right where I am meant to be and that I am not alone.

The Granny Trail

Many years ago, probably thirty or more, the Andrada Ranch in Vail ran their cattle on what was then State land around our home. Across the street, there were about thirty acres of undeveloped land the cattle traveled on to get to the big tanks north of us on State land. These manmade tanks were a real feat. Great berms of earth were created to catch the flow of water off the Andrada Wash thus creating a pond or tank.

Over the course of time the cattle developed little trails they followed year after year on the way to the tank for water and grazing. On the acreage across the street from us was one of those trails. We rode on the trail for years on horseback wandering here and there through little arroyos and rambling around cacti and trees. We called it "bush whacking" because it made the ride more interesting. There's nothing in horsemanship more boring than riding on a straight line.

My mother Helen Stowers died March 29, 2004. After the cremation my sister Patti mailed me a little wooden box with some of mother's ashes. I wanted to have a little ceremony to honor my mother and to dedicate an Ocotillo cactus in her name seemed appropriate. When our family first relocated to Tucson one of the local gas stations with a fill up gave you a tall cacti decorated frosty iced tea glass identifying by name each cactus. Mother loved the ocotillo from the beginning. So it only seemed appropriate we locate one for the ceremony.

    I wrote a little poem for her and collected red rose blossoms, her favorite, to scatter around the cactus. Bill and I saddled our horses and ponied a third. I attached her high school class ring to the saddle horn and in the stirrups attached my boots backward in the horseless rider tradition seen in funeral parades. We rode to the location and scattered mother's ashes and rose petals around her favorite ocotillo. After reading the poem I named the trail the Granny Trail in her honor. She frequently told the story of Prince the work horse on her father's farm she got to ride and I would like to believe that she would be pleased with our little ceremony. Now mother is scattered at sea in the Baja and in the Sonoran Desert in Arizona, her two favorite places.

Bill and I are no longer riding but occasionally I still walk the Granny Trail just to walk by mother's ocotillo to say hello.

Follow the Path with Heart

When I look back over the people who were significant in my life, my adventures, my humor and my accomplishments I realize I have had a magnificent and exciting journey on my path. Seventy-two is a perfect age for winding things up. Then again, maybe not. However, a wise man once told me, "Follow the Path with Heart" and the universe opens up and pulls you along.

It is my belief that everyone needs a passion for living in their lives otherwise hope can be lost. My adventures took me to places I wanted to go and to people I wanted to see. My accomplishments showed me what I was made of. Some were very challenging and painful but most of them an adventure. But with every path with heart comes an ending and a void is left to be filled. The saying goes, "When one door closes another one opens."

After thirteen years of horseback riding with Bill my last fall at age 68 told me it was time to hang up my spurs. I grieved this passion for at least two years. A friend told me that right around the corner awaits your next passion. She was right. I enrolled in my first Zumba class. I love to dance which started when I was five. At sixty-eight it was difficult at first but I picked up the routines and danced for two and a half years until my hip joints had other ideas. I had to hang up my dance shoes. I grieved that for at least two years.

I asked myself, "How could anything equal horseback riding and Zumba dancing?" Another void to be filled. I remembered what my friend told me about the next passion right around the corner. She was right; this time my estranged son Tommy came back into my life before he died. Seeing him again more than filled the void the others left behind. Talk about grief! I'm still grieving and probably will for the rest of my life. It gets better but now I had another void.

That's when I was inspired to write my memoires. Little by little the Path with Heart has evolved one chapter at a time. Looking back over my life has not been a disappointment at all. In fact it has been downright fascinating. I love writing because I don't have to leave the house, I can get up and get a cup of coffee, make a snack, or go to the bathroom. I can even write in my pajamas. Getting to be seventy-two is just the beginning of the next chapter of my path with heart.

Copyright © 2017 by Pamela Stowers Cunningham

www.ingramcontent.com/pod-product-compliance
Lightning Source LLC
Chambersburg PA
CBHW071451040426
42444CB00008B/1289